The Unvarnished Jesus

A Lenten Journey

By Brian Zahnd

The Unvarnished Jesus:
A Lenten Journey

Copyright 2019 by Brian Zahnd
www.brianzahnd.com

Published by Spello Press

ISBN-13: 978-0-9668421-0-4

In memory of Eugene Peterson (1932–2018), a beautiful soul who helped me on my journey, encouraged me in my writing, and will always be my model for what a pastor should be.

Introduction to
The Unvarnished Jesus

In February of 2006 I was in New Delhi, India staying in the Imperial Hotel. I had just concluded a conference for a thousand pastors in Orissa and I had a couple of days to relax in my favorite hotel in one of my favorite cities in the world before the long journey home. During my two days at the Imperial Hotel I was working on a new sermon series. At this point I was two years into a very significant spiritual and theological transition. After nearly twenty-five years of pastoral ministry I was encountering Jesus in new ways that posed profound challenges to many of the assumptions I had grown comfortable with. The Jesus I was discovering in midlife was a challenge to the con-sumerism, Americanism, militarism, and individualism that had come to characterize so much of the Christianity

I knew. This period of my life is what some describe as deconstruction, but I never thought of it that way or used that term. I tended to talk about what I was experiencing as having new eyes—I told my church repeatedly that with my new eyes the Bible I had been reading for decades had become a new book. Or with a more brazen rhetorical flourish I would say I was moving beyond easy-cheesy-cotton-candy-Christianity .Eventually I settled on Jesus turning water to wine at Cana as my preferred metaphor. A re-engagement with Jesus caused a weak, watery, diluted Christianity to be transformed into something rich, robust, and intoxicating. In midlife, instead of the party being over, it was just getting started. It was like being born again again.

I was thrilled with the discoveries I was making, but I also wanted to bring people along with me on this exciting new journey, because that's what pastors are supposed to do. And so I was outlining a series of sermons where I would try to present Jesus in an non-domesticated way. I called the series "The Unvarnished Jesus" because in those sermons I was attempting to remove the layers of lacquer comprised of the cultural assumptions that prevent us from seeing just how challenging and compelling Jesus really is.

On my second day at the Imperial working on these sermons I was suddenly overwhelmed by a wave of anxiety. I knew the sermons would be good, but they would also be dangerous. Presenting Jesus without a certain amount of mitigating varnish to an American church is not safe. I was plagued with thoughts like: How will this go over? How will the congregation react? Who's going to get mad and leave the church over this? I had to decide what I was going to do, so I left the hotel and went for a long walk through the streets of New Delhi, praying and trying to recover my nerve. When I returned to the hotel I had made up my mind—I would preach the unvarnished Jesus as honestly as I could, come what may. I knew it was a pivotal moment. I even took a picture of my Bible, notes, and laptop sitting on the desk to memorialize the decision I'd made to preach Jesus without varnish. I often looked at that picture, and when I do I feel the thrill and anxiety all over again. Those two days in the Imperial Hotel were a crucial turning point for me and for our church.

On the long flight home I read *Step Across This Line*—a collection of essays by the Indian-born writer Salman Rushdie. In his essay on the Taj Mahal I came across this paragraph.

The problem with the Taj Mahal is that it has become so overlaid with accumulated meanings as to be almost impossible to see. When you arrive at the outer walls of the gardens in which the Taj is set, it's as if every hustler and hawker in Agra is waiting for you to make the familiarity-breeds-contempt problem worse, peddling imitation Mahals of every size and price. This leads to a certain amount of shoulder-shrugging disenchantment. Recently, a British friend who was about to make his first visit to India told me that he had decided to leave the Taj off his itinerary because of its over-exposure. If I urged him not to, it's because of my own vivid memory of pushing my way for the first time through the jostling crowd of imitation-vendors, past all the myriad hawkers of meaning and interpretation, and into the presence of *the thing itself*, which utterly overwhelmed me, and made all my notions about its devaluation feel totally and completely redundant. The building itself left my skepticism in shreds. Announcing itself as itself, insisting with absolute force on its sovereign authority, it simply obliterated the million million counterfeits of it and glowingly filled, once and forever, the place in the mind previously occupied by its mulacra.

That was it! That was exactly what I wanted to do with "The Unvarnished Jesus." I wanted a Jesus who had been overlaid with so many accumulated meanings as to be impossible to see to once again announce himself as himself with the absolute force of sovereign authority and obliterate the million million counterfeits! Over the next two months I preached "The Unvarnished Jesus" sermons and wrote an Unvarnished Jesus blog post every day for sixty-one days. It was a turning point for our church. We were headed in the right direction, but it would be a difficult road; as Jesus said, "the gate is narrow and the road is hard that leads to life." We lost a lot of people over the next few years because an unvarnished Jesus who refuses to be a spokesperson for the assumed cultural values of Americanism is deeply unsettling for many American Christians. But the water turned to wine and we eventually arrived at a beautiful place, and if I had it to do all over again I wouldn't change a thing. (This is the story I tell in my memoir, *Water To Wine*.)

This book of daily Lenten reflections is not a replication of those sermons and blogs from fourteen years ago, but they are written in the same spirit. Lent is a forty-six day period prior to Easter (forty days of some kind of fasting with six Sunday feasts) during which we follow Jesus from Galilee to Jerusalem where he establishes the kingdom of God through his death, burial, and resurrection. To help you make the most of the season of Lent I've provided a Gospel reading and a brief reflection on Jesus for each day. The Sunday selections are taken from one of the Gospel readings in the three-year cycle of the Revised Common Lectionary. The other forty readings are my own selections, all taken from the second half of Jesus' ministry—first from Mark, followed by Matthew, Luke, and John. Then there is a two-week journey through the fourteen Scriptural Stations of the Cross. Our Lenten journey concludes with daily readings and reflections through the events of

Holy Week. Each Lenten reflection concludes with a brief prayer addressed to our Lord. So I invite you to join me on a pilgrimage—a forty-six day journey from Ash Wednesday to Holy Saturday in a quest to encounter the unvarnished Jesus.

DAY 1

Feb 26

ASH WEDNESDAY

Mark 8:31– 38

Jesus Foretells His Death

We begin our Lenten journey with Jesus by hearing him tell us that he's not headed to greatness as the world esteems greatness, but to the cross and to death. Peter and the rest of the disciples understand that Jesus is on his way to the capital city of Jerusalem to lay claim to the throne—to become the King of the Jews. But without any ambiguity Jesus tells his disciples that he will suffer many things, be rejected by the chief priests, and finally be killed. Yes, Jesus also says that his apparent defeat will be turned to victory when he is raised on the third day, but his disciples probably hear this as an idiom referring to the resurrection of the righteous at some point in the future—as when Hosea says, "After two days he will revive us; on the third day

9

he will raise us up." That Jesus could become King of the Jews *through* suffering and death is inconceivable to Peter. For Peter, a messiah who is killed is a messiah who fails, and Peter didn't sign up for failure. Jesus alone seems to understand that a breakthrough into new life is only attained through the experience of loss. Martin Luther was right, Christianity is not a theology of glory, but a theology of the cross. But to choose the way of the cross over the way of glory is a hard lesson to learn.

Like Peter, we also may be inclined to argue with Jesus when he calls us to choose the way of the cross. "Surely not, Jesus! I don't want to suffer and lose, I want to be great and win!" But Jesus calls that kind of thinking satanic! As the book of Proverbs says, "There is a way that seems right to a person, but its end is the way to death." Most of us are scripted to think that life is a game and the purpose of life is to win. This is the way that *seems* right. But the divine truth is that life is a gift and the purpose of life is to learn to love well.

And so Jesus invites us to follow him, not in a march to greatness, but in the cross-carrying way of self-denial. This and this alone is the way of true discipleship. It's also the way to abundant life. Grasping for greatness is the way of the rat race. But as Walter Brueggemann says, the problem with the rat race is that even if you win, you're still a rat. Or as Jesus put it, what do you gain if you win it all, but lose your soul? During this season of Lent let's renew our commitment to take up our cross and follow Jesus!

Lord Jesus, we are so often afraid that the way of the cross leads only to loss—a loss that we fear we cannot bear. Help us to believe you and to embrace the cross as the way that ultimately leads to authentic love and abundant life. Amen.

DAY 2 Feb 27

THURSDAY

Mark 10:17–31
Jesus and the Rich Young Ruler

The story of Jesus and the Rich Young Ruler is very interesting. Matthew, Mark, and Luke all tell this story but each with a subtle difference. Yet it's the subtle difference in each of the synoptic Gospels that really helps us get to the heart of this story. In telling the rich young ruler what he needs to do to participate in the life of the kingdom of God, Jesus summarizes the final six decrees of the Ten Commandments. The first four of the Ten Commandments are intended to form Israel in right relationship with God, or what we call worship. The final six commandments are intended to form Israel in right relationship with one another, or what we call justice. The most ambiguous of the ten commandments is the last: "You shall not covet." What does that mean?

What does it mean not to covet? This is where the subtle differences in the three Gospel accounts of the story of Jesus and the rich young ruler help us to understand what is intended by, "You shall not covet."

In Mark's Gospel, Jesus doesn't say, "Do not covet," but instead says, "Do not defraud." In other words, the tenth commandment is interpreted by Jesus as "do not defraud." Jesus, John the Baptist, and James the brother of Jesus all emphasized economic justice. They taught that if we covet a second coat when our brother has none, we have in some way defrauded our brother. There is a certain amount of wealth that *belongs* to every human being. As the early church father Ambrose of Milan (340–397) said, "You are not making a gift of your possession to a poor person. You are handing over to him what is his."

In Matthew's Gospel, when Jesus counsels the rich young ruler, the commandment from Exodus, "You shall not covet," is replaced with the command from Leviticus that says, "Love your neighbor as yourself." Coveting (which is the engine of capitalism) places us in economic competition with our neighbors and makes it very difficult for us to engage in neighborly love.

When we're in competition with our neighbors it's hard to love them.

In Luke's gospel, the tenth commandment is not mentioned at all, in order to emphasize that this is the one thing the young man lacks. The rich young ruler does not have a problem with murder, adultery, theft, lying, or dishonoring his parents; his problem lies with the tenth commandment—a commandment that broaches upon the thorny issue of economic self-interest.

The truth is that for most of us economic self-interest is the single greatest obstacle to full participation in the kingdom of God. We cannot love our neighbor as our self without being willing to share our wealth.

Lord Jesus, we have bought the lie that we cannot afford to be generous; we are afraid that we will come up short. Help us to remember that when we seek first your kingdom and your justice, all that we need will be provided for us. Amen.

Feb 28

DAY 3

FRIDAY

Mark 10:32–45

James and John Make A Request of Jesus

Jesus and his disciples are on their way to the capital city of Jerusalem where Jesus is to be crowned King of the Jews. James and John are eager to have prominent positions in Jesus' kingdom—they want to be on his right and on his left. Let's say it this way: James and John want to be Secretary of State and Secretary of Defense in the new administration. But Jesus tells them they don't know what they're asking. Why? Because who *was* on Jesus' right and left as he entered the glory of his kingdom? It was the two revolutionaries who were crucified with him! The glory of the kingdom is

17

Jesus Christ crucified and James and John had unwittingly asked to be crucified with Jesus. This should remind us that the kingdom of Christ does not come in the way of worldly power politics.

The kingdom of Christ is the anti-Rome and Jesus is the anti-Caesar. Caesar and all his successors come to power through conquest. But Jesus became King of Kings on Good Friday. Jesus eternally reigns from the cross. They way of Christ is not the way of conquest and colonialism, but the way of co-suffering love. James and John were still laboring under the ancient lie that the only way to really change the world is through the force of violent power. And I'm afraid that most of us are still very susceptible to this lie. We think of love as mere sentiment, while accepting violence as true power. Yet the whole life and ministry of Jesus is a reputation of this lie.

When the other disciples learned how James and John were jockeying for positions of prominence in the coming kingdom, they were indignant at the two brothers. So Jesus explained to his disciples that though the way of empire is to seek domination, "it shall not be so among you." The kingdom of God is a kingdom of love, not domination. As followers of Jesus we are called to the practice of radical patience, because the kingdom of God is without coercion. We persuade by love, witness, Spirit, reason, rhetoric, and if need be, by martyrdom, but never by force. This is what Alan Kreider described as "the patient ferment of the early church."

And this is why the early church—the church prior to Constantine and Christendom—had a deep ambivalence to the machinations of imperial politics. The early church understood that the kingdom of God did not and could not come through Caesar or the ways of Caesar, thus they had no ambition to wield the power of Caesar's sword. There is no such thing as a Christlike Caesar—there is only Christ and his cross. May we remember this today.

Lord Jesus, forgive us for imagining that your kingdom can come by the way of Caesar and the politics of coercion. Help us to become a patient people who renounce the sword and take up the cross. Amen.

DAY 4

SATURDAY

Feb 25

Mark 10:46–52

Jesus Heals Bartimaeus

Mark tells us that as Jesus was making his final approach to Jerusalem he came to Jericho and then immediately left Jericho. In Mark's Gospel Jesus was about to pass right through Jericho with nothing happening. But when the blind beggar Bartimaeus heard that it was Jesus, the miracle-worker from Galilee, who was passing by, he began to plead for mercy. With a bold determination that he be heard, the beggar began to cry, "Jesus, Son of David, have mercy on me!" This calls to mind a well-known hymn by the famous American songwriter Fanny Crosby, who like Bartimaeus was also blind.

Pass me not, O gentle Savior,

21

Hear my humble cry;

While on others thou art calling,

Do not pass me by.

When the crowd rebuked Bartimaeus for his outburst, he was not deterred, but cried out all the more. The result was that Jesus stopped, called for him, and healed him. Bartimaeus then joined those who were following Jesus up to Jerusalem. I like to imagine the healed beggar among the crowd of Passover pilgrims waving a palm branch and shouting "Hosanna!" as Jesus entered the city.

Most of us could stand to be a bit more like Bartimaeus. As we continue in our Christian life we may experience enough disappointments in prayer that we slip into praying safe prayers—prayers that never risk disappointment. We no longer pray boldly like Bartimaeus; instead we pray careful prayers—prayers that are so vague and ambiguous that we would be hard-pressed to tell whether or not they were ever answered. I understand this inclination and there have been times in my own life when I have slipped into praying this way. But if we never actually ask Jesus to specifically and definably intervene in our life, though we may shield ourselves from disappointment, we also preclude the possibility of experiencing a miracle. We need to risk disappointment in prayer.

If we ask Jesus to specifically act in our life, we may indeed experience some disappointment if our prayer is not answered as we hoped. But Jesus can help us to bear that disappointment and the Spirit can alert us to unanticipated ways in which God is at work in our lives. But if we abandon all expectations in prayer, we surrender to a modern skepticism that leaves our lives a barren and sterile landscape devoid of divine presence and intervention. I can live in a world where not all of my prayers are answered. But I cannot live in a world where a prayer-answering God is never called upon and thus absent. Today let's resolve to pray more boldly like Bartimaeus and defy the cynical crowd that would rebuke us for actually thinking that Jesus would respond to our cry for mercy.

Lord Jesus Christ, Son of God, have mercy on us. We are needy people and we need you to help us, to heal us, to rescue us. Merciful Savior, hear our prayer today and show us your salvation. Amen.

DAY 5
SUNDAY

Mark ?

Matthew 4:1–11
Jesus Is Tempted In the Wilderness

Prior to his public ministry Jesus spent forty days in the wilderness in prayer and fasting. During this time he was tempted by the devil. But how did the devil come to Jesus? Did he come wearing a red suit, sporting horns and a forked tail, carrying a pitchfork? Did he say, "Hi, I'm the devil. I'm here to tempt you. Shall we begin?" Of course not. The devil came to Jesus the same way the devil comes to us—disguised as our own thoughts. As Jesus considered the course of his ministry, the devil tempted him to compromise the integrity of his mission. Jesus couldn't be tempted by overt evil, so the devil tempted him with a trilogy of "good ideas."

The three good ideas suggested by the devil were to feed everyone, persuade everyone, and liberate everyone. And who could disagree with these ideas? They seem like good ideas. But there's a devil lurking in those good ideas, a devil that Jesus discerned.

The first temptation is to feed everyone...but forget about God. This is the temptation to make the kingdom of God solely about social justice. Yes, Jesus will multiply loaves and fishes and feed the hungry, but he will also say, "eat my flesh and drink my blood." We cannot achieve the second commandment to love our neighbor as our self if we bypass the first commandment to love God with all our heart.

The second temptation is to persuade everyone, and thereby eliminate faith. This is the temptation to prove God empirically—either by miracles or by science—and thus remove the need for faith. The capacity to believe or doubt is what creates space for us be free and authentic beings, and not mere robots controlled by God. As Frederick Buechner says, "If there were no room for doubt, there would be no room for me."

The third temptation is the most subtle of all. It's the temptation to liberate everyone...and kill the bad guys. This is the temptation to bypass the cross and seize Caesar's sword. The third "good idea" is the temptation to reach for the ring of power. *One ring to rule them all, one ring to find them, one ring to bring them all, and in the darkness bind them.* This is the temptation to justify the means by the end. But Jesus understood that the means are the end in the process of becoming. Jesus perceived that to justify violent means by an imagined good end is to worship the devil!

The unvarnished Jesus cannot be empirically proved or reduced to a spokesperson for a preferred ism. Jesus will not be the poster boy for left-wing activism or right-wing militarism. Jesus has his own agenda—it's just and peaceable, but first of all it worships God.

Lord Jesus, you are the wisdom of God. Lead us not into the realm of temptation, but deliver us from the evil of the devil's "good ideas." Jesus, you are the Word of God by whom we overcome the evil one. Amen.

DAY 6

Mar 3

MONDAY

Matthew 17:14–21

Jesus Heals A Demon-Possessed Boy

As far as I'm concerned faith is more than a bit of a mystery—especially if we're talking about faith that moves mountains and does the impossible. The prosperity gospel has given millions of Christians a very distorted understanding of both God and faith. God is not a divine vending machine dispensing desired outcomes in exchange for the right amount of faith currency. God is not a machine and faith is not a medium of exchange. God and faith are much more complex than this.

Nevertheless Jesus says that faith like a mustard seed moves us beyond what we think are the limits of what is possible. But what does it mean to have faith like a mustard seed? Is it just the tiniest bit of faith? I

29

don't think so. Jesus talked about mustard seeds on other occasions, saying that even though the mustard seed is the smallest seed, it can grow into the biggest plant in the garden. Yes, mustard seeds are small, but they possess the capacity for tremendous growth. Faith is not a commodity or a currency—it's not a coin to operate a vending machine. Faith is organic, living, and capable of growth. Faith is like a seed, not a coin.

The model for faith given to us in the Bible is Abraham. The Apostle Paul describes Abraham as "the father of all who have faith." It's interesting to consider that though Abraham is the father of faith, he may have never known "faith" as a word. For Abraham faith was not an abstract concept, but the orientation of his soul toward God. Faith was how he lived his life in relationship with the invisible God who called him out of Ur and who made impossible promises—promises that came to pass over the course of a lifetime. Abraham did not become the father of faith by accumulating a currency of faith; rather faith grew in Abraham's life until it was the most dominant reality in the garden of his soul.

Though we could speak of *doing* the impossible, I think it's better to speak of *becoming* what we once thought was impossible. The emphasis should always be on becoming over doing. At one point in his life Abraham thought it was impossible for him to become a father—it was so impossible that he laughed at the thought of it. But through faith that's exactly what he became. The seed of faith grew in Abraham's life until one day he became what he had previously assumed was impossible.

Today you may feel that it is impossible for you to become the kind of person whose life is defined by faith, hope, and love. But stay on the journey, keep your soul oriented toward God, give faith time and space to grow, and eventually you will become what you once that was impossible.

Lord Jesus, our faith is small, but we do not despair. May our faith in you be like a mustard seed, that though small, grows and grows until we become what we once thought impossible. Amen.

DAY 7

Mary (handwritten)

TUESDAY

Matthew 17:24–27

Jesus and the Temple Tax

This delightful story has several things going on. First of all, Jesus anticipates and answers Peter's question about the half-shekel temple tax before Peter can ask it. But in the typical manner of a Jewish rabbi his answer to Peter's question comes in the form of his own question—a question with an obvious answer: kings collect taxes from others, not from their sons. This is Jesus making an implicit claim to be the Son of God.

But we also see that Jesus has a rather ambivalent attitude toward the temple. Jesus knows that the time of the temple era is drawing to a close and even predicts its destruction. (When Jesus talks about the "end" in the Olivet Discourse, he isn't talking about the end of the world, but about the end of the temple and the temple age.) And during his final week of ministry Jesus will stage a fiery protest in the temple to expose priestly corruption. But Jesus doesn't denounce the temple itself. Jesus is not an opponent of religion in the manner of Voltaire or Nietzsche as so many moderns imagine. Jesus often spoke favorably of the temple and he and his disciples participated in the various temple rites. To offend people over the temple itself was not something Jesus was interested in, so he was content to pay the half-shekel temple tax for himself and Peter.

But it's how the temple tax is paid that makes the story so delightful—from a shekel coin found in a fish's mouth! People who followed Jesus always found that there was somehow more than enough. Water turned into wine, loaves and fish multiplied, and money for a tax bill was found in a fish's mouth. Jesus taught his disciples not to worry about provision. When we seek first the kingdom of God, what we need will be provided. This promise is not an idle theory to me—I've proved it over and over again.

When Peri and I first began Word of Life Church in the early 1980s, we had no money at all. Our fledgling congregation consisted almost entirely of people with no money, Peri was in nursing school, and my salary was $90 a week. We had to live by faith. It wasn't an easy time, but we can tell stories of God's provision that are no less miraculous than finding a coin in a fish's mouth! Though I wouldn't want to go back to those days, I wouldn't trade our experience of living by faith for anything.

There's a fish restaurant near the Sea of Galilee that will place a shekel coin in the mouth of a grilled St. Peter's fish. I like that. It's a whimsical reminder that when we walk with Jesus we can expect to be surprised by miracles of provision.

Lord Jesus, we are often so anxious about money; help us to remember what you taught about trusting God. Jesus, when we don't have enough we look to you to be our provider. Amen.

DAY 8

March 5 (handwritten)

WEDNESDAY

Matthew 18:10–14
Jesus Gives the Parable of
the Lost Sheep

We live in a world gone wrong and our broken world likes to divide the world into big people and little people. The rich and famous are big people. The important and influential are big people. This person is big in business and that person is a really big star. That's how we talk. We are enamored by what is big—especially in America where bigness is part of our national religion. It's this strange longing for bigness that is mocked in Counting Crows' song *Mr. Jones*—

> *When I look at the television,*
> *I wanna see me*

Staring right back at me
We all wanna be big stars
But we don't know why,
and we don't know how

Then there's the vast majority—the little people. These are the masses of humanity often leading what Thoreau described as "lives of quiet desperation." These are the ones who are easily overlooked and usually dismissed as unimportant. In the religion of bigness these are the ones who count next to nothing. These are the uncredited extras in the movie of American life starring the big people.

But Jesus refuses to participate in our big/little sorting of people. Jesus tells us that we must not despise (think little of) the little ones. After the disciples inquired, "Who is the greatest in the kingdom of heaven," Jesus gave a parable about a shepherd who prioritizes a little lost lamb over all the rest. The good shepherd seeks out the lamb, not because it's big and important, but precisely because it's little, overlooked, and lost. Jesus tells us that his Father is deeply concerned that none of these little ones should be lost.

If our thinking about the kingdom of God is

infected with American notions of greatness and bigness, we will inevitably have a deeply distorted Christianity. We will in fact have a Christianity that pursues the very things that Jesus taught were fleeting and meaningless. It's this kind of distortion that gives rise to Christian celebrity culture. Yes, some Christians will gain notoriety, but it should be for Christlikeness, not for celebrity based on bigness. Bigness is not a Christian value. In the thirteenth century Saint Francis of Assisi was one of the most well-known people in Europe, but he was famous for his poverty, his humility, his peaceableness, his Christlikeness. This is a far cry from being a big star in Christian celebrity culture.

Today let's remember to pay attention to the little ones around us. Seek them out. Lift them up. Give them the grace of being seen, heard, and respected. Let us alert the overlooked to the dignity that is theirs by virtue of being a child of God.

Lord Jesus, forgive us for trying to be big when you call us to be humble. Help us to seek out and pay attention to those who are most often overlooked among us. Help us to be good shepherds to lost sheep. Amen.

DAY 9 ~~March~~

THURSDAY

Matthew 18:21–35
Jesus Gives the Parable of the
Unforgiving Servant

Today we read about Jesus famously telling us that we are to forgive seventy times seven. In response to Peter's apparently generous suggestion that forgiveness be extended seven times, Jesus multiplies forgiveness to seventy times seven. He then gives a remarkable parable where a servant is forgiven a preposterous debt of ten thousand talents. A talent was a monetary unit worth about twenty years' wages for a laborer; thus ten thousand talents would be equivalent to two million years' wages or tens of billions of dollars! Jesus has cast his parable on forgiveness in the theater of the absurd to make his point.

But what I find most interesting about this

parable is how Jesus recycles the seventy times seven equation. This equation first appears in Genesis when a man named Lamech composed this bloody limerick—

> I have killed a man for wounding me,
> A young man for striking me.
> If Cain's vengeance is sevenfold,
> Then my vengeance is seventy times sevenfold.

According to the genealogy in Genesis, Lamech was the great-great-great-grandson of Cain—the first murderer. Cain introduced killing and Lamech threatened to multiply lethal vengeance seventy times seven. Lamech's insane commitment to revenge led to the exponential violence in the days of Noah one generation later. Though we often imagine other lurid sins, violence is the only sin mentioned in the text. In the Genesis story it was human violence spiraling out of control that grieved the heart of God and led to the divine judgment of the deluge. We should take this warning to heart. In an age where the killing capacity of Cain's club has been exponentially multiplied by the creation of nuclear arsenals, searching for Noah's ark on Mount Ararat instead of seeking to rid the world of violence really is an exercise in missing the point!

Long after the days of Noah, Moses sought to mitigate Lamech-like revenge to a reciprocal level by restricting violent retaliation to "an eye for an eye and a tooth for a tooth." This was a step in the right direction, but it was hardly an adequate solution for the problem of violence. As Gandhi shrewdly observed, "an eye for an eye leaves the whole world blind." In a world where the capacity to unleash lethal violence is now beyond comprehension we need something better than tit-for-tat retaliation. "Nuclear strike for nuclear strike" will leave the world a smoldering hellscape.

And so the Savior of the world directs us toward a re-appropriation of Lamech's seventy time seven equation, applying it to the practice of radical forgiveness. The most remarkable thing about Christ-informed ethics is its commitment to forgiveness—indeed, if Christianity is about anything, it's about forgiveness. So Jesus calls us beyond the ever-escalating revenge of Lamech and beyond the mitigated revenge of Moses into a world where revenge is renounced altogether. Jesus saves the world by turning exponential revenge into exponential forgiveness.

Lord Jesus, you call us not to a mitigation of revenge or even to sevenfold forgiveness, but to the seventy times seven practice of radical forgiveness. Give us grace to forgive as we have been forgiven. Amen.

DAY 10

FRIDAY

Mt 21 7

Matthew 19:13–15
Jesus Blesses the Children

Peri and I raised three sons. They're all grown now and today we have seven grandchildren—all under the age of nine. My seven young grandchildren provide focus for what I want to do in pastoral ministry. Everyday I pray this prayer: "God, help me to help make Christianity possible for my grandchildren and their generation." If we want Christian faith to survive in a secular age we have to figure out how to form Christian faith in little children. In today's Scripture reading we see that Jesus always has time to lay his hands on little children and bless them, as we hear him famously say, "Let the little children come to me and do not hinder them."

As passé as it may sound to cynical ears, if we want faith in Jesus to remain realistically possible in a secular age, one of the most valuable things we can do is bring children to church. We need to raise children in the community that is formed and sustained by the grand narrative of Scripture—a story that culminates in the gospel of Jesus Christ. In an irreligious culture where not much is sacred, we need to introduce children to the sacred place where sacrament is formative and faith is normative. Christian faith cannot long be sustained as a private opinion held by a lone individual. Christianity is not a solo project. Even though you may stubbornly maintain some kind of faith in Jesus without belonging to a church, your children probably will not, and your grandchildren almost certainly will not. One of the essential tasks of the church is to pass on the faith from one generation to another, and without the church this is nearly impossible. If we're interested in our children and grandchildren sharing our faith, we need the church.

The church in Western culture (in contrast with the global South) is in rapid decline. In North America young people are fleeing fundamentalist churches ensnared in culture war causes and historic churches plagued with abuse scandals. I understand this. But this is not the whole story. There are healthy churches out there led by sincere humble people doing good work. For the sake of our children and grandchildren we need to help these churches survive. In my own ministry I've noticed that young people who were sure they were done with the church often begin to have second thoughts when they have their own children. It turns out they *are* interested in their children knowing about Jesus, not just as a historical figure, but as the Lord worshipped by the church. A world without Jesus is really not appealing. Sometimes "Dones" give the church a second chance when they begin to look at the world through the eyes of their children. So we need churches where parents can bring their children to a living Christ who still receives and blesses them. Today you might want to ask Jesus what you can do to help make Christian faith possible for future generations. I can't think of anything more important.

Lord Jesus, in a secular age we seek to live as keepers of the sacred. Help us by your grace to pass on sacred gifts to the generations who come after us. Amen.

DAY 11 *Mar 8*

SATURDAY

Matthew 20:1–16
Jesus Gives the Parable of the
Workers in the Vineyard

The parable of the laborers in the vineyard may be Jesus' most scandalous parable—at least for Americans formed in the cowboy myth of rugged individualism. If told this parable came from anyone else, most American Christians would dismiss it as Marxist propaganda. But there it is, right in the middle of the Gospel of Matthew, a parable from Jesus featuring a radical egalitarianism that will no doubt offend the sensibilities of a convinced capitalist. What this parable reveals is how *unlike* the kingdom of God most of us tend to be in our thinking and especially in our economics. We are never more prone to put a softening varnish on Jesus than when he broaches the subject of money.

In this parable Jesus says that the kingdom of heaven is like a person who worked only one hour being paid the same as a person who worked all day. Think about that. In the story a group of people worked all day and received a fair wage for a day's work. But another group of people worked only one hour and received the same wage. We deride that as welfare. We're convinced it's inequitable. We call it unfair. But Jesus calls it the kingdom of heaven! The kingdom of heaven is not a meritocracy; the kingdom of heaven is an economy of grace. The vineyard owner (who obviously represents God) was more interested in giving people what they needed than giving them what they deserved—and he was willing to do so at his own expense. The only person who suffers loss in this parable is the vineyard owner. In this story no one is cheated. The anger of the group paid last was based not in any injustice they had suffered, but in their own envious resentment. The group paid first simply received what they *needed* based solely on the extravagant generosity of the vineyard owner. The vineyard owner didn't want any of his workers going hungry, no matter how long they had or had not worked. The parable of the workers in the vineyard is designed by Jesus to provoke the pharisaical ire of those who believe they deserve the love of God more than others. In this regard the parable of the laborers in the vineyard is a cousin to the more palatable parable of the prodigal son.

If we fear that someone we deem as less deserving than us will be made equal to us based on their need and God's love, we're still operating according to an economy outside the kingdom of heaven. Or more tellingly, why do we tend to read ourselves into the story as laborers who worked all day? Why are we so convinced of our own deservedness? Isn't it just as likely that in the sight of God we are those who though only laboring one hour still need—not deserve, but *need*—a day's wage? Ask yourself this question: Am I sustained by the law of just deserts or by the grace of God?

Lord Jesus, help us not to be offended at the scandalous grace by which we are all saved; may we be more like your Apostle Paul who saw himself as the chief of sinners saved by grace. Amen.

51

DAY 12 *Mar 9*
SUNDAY

Matthew 17:1–9
Jesus Is Transfigured

The Transfiguration of Jesus Christ on Mount Tabor is the crescendo of his Galilean ministry and marks the point where Jesus begins his long death march to Jerusalem. As Jesus comes down from the top of the mountain he speaks to Peter, James, and John about his impending death—something he had revealed to his disciples only six days earlier. After the Transfiguration the music score in the gospel story changes from a major to a minor key. Lent is a season of walking with Jesus toward his coronation by crucifixion.

One of the more fascinating aspects of the Transfiguration is the mysterious appearance of two titans from the Old Testament who lived centuries before Jesus—Moses and Elijah. Of course with Moses as the law-giver and Elijah as the prototypical prophet they represent the Old Testament itself—Moses and Elijah are the Law and the Prophets. In his sermon on the Mount Jesus announced that he had come to fulfill the Law and the Prophets. What the Law and the Prophets had aimed for but had never fully attained, Jesus would accomplish. It is Jesus Christ, not Moses and Elijah, who fully inaugurates the kingdom of God. The Mount of Transfiguration is where Moses and Elijah find their successor and bear witness that it is the Christ who will complete what they had begun.

In the Stygian darkness of the pagan world the Law and the Prophets enabled the Hebrew people to grope forward in the understanding of who God is. The Law and the Prophets are the moon and stars that enabled Israel to navigate a treacherous world of idolatry and injustice. But when the day dawns, the moon and stars recede and give way to the rising sun. Jesus Christ is the sun of righteousness risen with healing in his rays, and Moses and Elijah have come to Tabor to bear witness to the greatness of the Son of God.

Simon Peter seems to have missed this symbolism, thinking instead of erecting three shrines—one for Moses, one for Elijah, and one for Jesus. But this idea of making the Law and the Prophets equal to Christ is quickly shot down when the voice from the cloud says, "This is my beloved Son with whom I am well pleased. Listen to him!" Jesus is what God has to say. A flat reading of the Bible allows us to proof-text any idea we want, but Jesus is the Word of God.

So if Moses says to practice capital punishment and stone certain sinners, Jesus says, "Let the one without sin cast the first stone," and God says, "This is my beloved Son. Listen to him!" Or if Elijah calls down fire from heaven to consume the soldiers sent to arrest him, Jesus says, "Love your enemies," and God says, "This is my beloved Son. Listen to him!" Wars of conquest, capital punishment, violent retribution, the institution of slavery, and women held as property are all "biblical," but when seen in the light brighter than the sun shining from the face of Christ, everything must be re-evaluated because Jesus is what God has to say!

Lord Jesus, you are the Word of the Father; you are the perfect revelation of who God is. May we learn to see all things in the light of your glorious countenance. Amen.

DAY 13 *Mar 9*

MONDAY

Luke 9:51–56

Jesus Is Rejected by a
Samaritan village

As Jesus begins his final journey to Jerusalem, he and his disciples are passing through Samaria. The Samaritans were a people related to the ancient Israelites of the Northern Kingdom. They had a shared history with the Judeans (Jews), but there were deep-seated hostilities between the two peoples based in religious differences and territorial disputes. The conflict between Jews and Samaritans in Jesus' day was not unlike the conflict between Israelis and Palestinians today. That Jesus engaged with Samaritans, healed Samaritans, and made Samaritans heroes in his parables would have been highly provocative to most Jews.

One of the points of religious dispute between Jews and Samaritans was about the proper location for ceremonial worship. The Jews said it was the temple in Jerusalem, while the Samaritans claimed it was the mountains of Samaria where the patriarchs had built their altars. As Jesus and his disciples passed through Samaria on their way to the feast of Passover in Jerusalem, they were refused hospitality in a Samaritan village because of this religious difference. James and John were so offended by this that they asked if they could call down fire from heaven and burn up the Samaritans. James and John pillaged the Bible to find warrant for their idea by citing the incident when Elijah twice called down fire from heaven and burned up a hundred soldiers sent from Samaria to arrest the prophet. What we see in today's Gospel reading is the "Sons of Thunder" (as Jesus aptly nicknamed them) trying to coerce the Prince of Peace into launching a drone strike on their enemies!

Yesterday we saw the Sons of Thunder on the Mount of Transfiguration. When the idea was floated that Jesus, Moses, and Elijah be treated equally, with a shrine for all three, the voice from heaven said, "This is my beloved Son. Listen to him!" But today James and

John have apparently forgotten what they heard on the holy mountain as they attempt to cite the actions of Elijah in order to get Jesus to act contrary to his Sermon on the Mount. Jesus was unimpressed and rebuked his disciples for an idea that, though "biblical," was completely contrary to the spirit of Jesus. Just because something is in the Bible doesn't necessarily mean it's a Christlike idea. Just because Elijah did it doesn't mean it's something followers of Jesus should do. Sometimes the Bible is like a Rorschach test, telling us more about ourselves than about God.

All Scripture is fulfilled in and by Jesus Christ. So if we don't see it in Jesus, we let it go—because even the Bible must bow to Jesus. If we read the Bible allowing it to do what it does best by pointing us to Jesus, we are engaging with Scripture properly. But if we read the Bible in search of texts to force Jesus to conform to our ideas about who to hate and how to justify violence, we can expect to be rebuked by the spirit of the living Christ.

Lord Jesus, you are greater than Moses and greater than Elijah, you are the very Son of God, the

Savior of the world. Help us to read Scripture in a way
that reveals your preeminence in all things. Amen.

DAY 14 ~Mar 10~

TUESDAY

Luke 10:25–37
Jesus Gives the Parable of the Good Samaritan

Yesterday we saw how James and John wanted Jesus to nuke a Samaritan village and how Jesus rebuked the Sons of Thunder for their biblically-inspired but un-Christlike idea. Today we see how Jesus makes a Samaritan the hero of one of his most famous parables. Jesus gives this parable in response to a question from a Torah scholar trying to wiggle out of loving his neighbor by asking for clarification on who actually constitutes a neighbor. The biblical scholar understood that Jesus had spoken correctly when he had identified love of God and love of neighbor as the heart of Scriptural revelation and the way that leads to life, but the scholar was looking for a loop-hole because there were obviously people he didn't want to love, and Samaritans would certainly have been on his not-to-be-loved list. Thus his lawyerly question. This is the backdrop for the parable of the Good Samaritan.

Jesus could have constructed his parable so that a noble Jew showed mercy to a Samaritan victim. This would have been a step in the right direction, but it would have kept the Jew in the superior role. Jesus' parable is more subversive than that. Jesus casts his parable so that a Jew is the victim, other Jews fail to act in love, and a compassionate Samaritan is the hero of the story. Jesus was challenging the Jewish tendency to look at Samaritans as two-dimensional villains. Jesus is essentially asking, "What are you going to do if the people whose theology you scorn are more merciful than you? What if the one you've made an outsider treats you as a neighbor, what are you going to do then?"

Alexander Solzhenitsyn, who came to faith in Christ amidst deep suffering in a Soviet gulag, said that the line that separates good and evil does not run between nationalities, ethnicities, religions, or political parties, but right through the heart of every person. Martin Buber taught us to stop relating to others as I-It, but as I-Thou—that is, we must learn to recognize the image of God in every other person. Rabbi Pinchas once asked his students how they could tell when the night had ended and the day had begun. One student suggested "Could it be when you can see an animal in the distance and tell whether it's a sheep or a dog?" "No," answered the rabbi. Another asked, "Is it when you can look at a tree in the distance and tell whether it's a fig tree or a date palm?" "No," answered the rabbi. "Then when is it?" the pupils demanded. Rabbi Pinchas said, "It is when you can look into the face of any person and recognize them as your sister or brother. Until we're able to do that, it is still night." Alexander Solzhenitsyn, Martin Buber, and Rabbi Pinchas had all mastered the lesson given to us by Jesus in the parable of the Good Samaritan. Who is my neighbor? The person I have an opportunity to love, help, and alleviate their suffering. The biblical text case for love of God is love of neighbor and the biblical test case for love of neighbor is love of enemy.

Lord Jesus, lead us in the way of life by teaching us how to recognize every person as our neighbor; and give us grace to engage with our neighbors in co-suffering love. Amen.

DAY 15

WEDNESDAY

Luke 10:38–42
Jesus, Mary, and Martha

The primary purpose of prayer is not to get God to do what we think God ought to do but to be properly formed. Toward this end we need both liturgical and contemplative forms of prayer. For years I've practiced and taught contemplative prayer as "sitting with Jesus." Two thousand years ago Mary of Bethany discovered that sitting with Jesus is the one thing that is necessary if we want to form our soul in the way of health and peace.

When Jesus came to Jerusalem he often stayed in the nearby village of Bethany as the guest of Lazarus, Martha and Mary. The family was wealthy and their large home could accommodate Jesus and his disciples.

On one occasion while Jesus was staying in their home, he was teaching his disciples while Martha was occupied—the text says she was distracted—in serving the guests. Breaking with the social norms and gender roles of the day, Mary did not assist her sister in serving the men, but sat at Jesus' feet as one of the disciples. When Martha in her irritation complained to Jesus and petitioned him to tell her sister to stop sitting and start serving, Jesus gently admonished Martha for being anxious and troubled about so many things and commended Mary for having chosen the one thing that is really necessary.

Martha, the busy sister, is well-intended, but her noble intentions aren't enough to prevent her from being anxious and troubled. Peace of mind is not the merited award for strict adherence to duty, but is a state cultivated through contemplative practices centered on Jesus. Isaiah said, "You will keep in perfect peace those whose minds are stayed on you." Without some form of contemplative practice we will spend too much time in one of three undesirable mental states: drifting back into the painful past, flitting about in the distracted present, or rushing ahead into the anxious future. Mary had learned the good practice—to sit with Jesus in the contemplative present. Without intentionally cultivating what Brother Lawrence called "the practice of the presence of God," our service for God will eventually become burdensome and will either be abandoned or carried out as an onerous duty.

In liturgical and personal prayer we use words to become properly formed and to present our petitions. But in contemplative prayer we sit silently acknowledging the presence of Christ. Each morning I initiate a time of sitting with Jesus with this prayer: *Christ I acknowledge you. Christ above me, very God of very God. Christ below me, incarnate of the earth. Christ before me when seen. Christ behind me when unseen. Christ at my right hand in my strength. Christ on my left in my weakness. Christ all around me filling all things everywhere with himself. Christ within me, formed by faith.* Then I simply sit with Jesus—for Jesus himself is salvation, peace, and healing. I pray that you too can find the transcendent peace that comes from learning to quietly sit with Jesus on a daily basis.

Lord Jesus, may the service we render to you not become a distraction to the one thing that is truly

necessary. Jesus, give us your peace as we sit with you.
Amen.

DAY 16

THURSDAY

Luke 16:19–31

Jesus Gives the Parable of the Rich Man and Lazarus

In the parable of the Rich Man and Lazarus, Jesus took a well-known Jewish folk tale (there are seven versions of it in rabbinic writings) about a rich man and a beggar who experience a dramatic reversal of fortunes upon death, and then adds a new twist to it— the part about the rich man's concern for his brothers. The effect of this new addition is to pull the story back into this present life. This parable is not primarily about the afterlife, but about how easy it is to miss the arrival of the kingdom of God if we overlook the poor and suffering who are all around us. In the previous chapter

Jesus gave the Pharisees the parable of the prodigal son—a story that ends with a dead brother coming back to life. Did the return of the prodigal son who "was dead and has come to life" convert the older brother (the Pharisees)? It did not. In the final scene, the older brother is outside the father's house gnashing his teeth in resentment and rage. The father has not sent his older son to the outer darkness, but in his refusal to forgive, the embittered brother has consigned himself to a self-imposed hell. If the Pharisees can't be converted to the way of love by listening to the Law and the Prophets, and by witnessing sinners coming to life through the ministry of Jesus, they won't be convinced even when a crucified Messiah is raised from the dead on the third day!

Jesus' teaching on hell is basically this: If you refuse to love, you cannot enter the kingdom of God and will end up a lonely tormented soul. If we take Jesus seriously as a teacher, we must never think the gospel is a means by which we can ignore God, scorn the suffering, mock the poor, and have everything turn out alright. If you want to know how to find hell, follow the path set by the rich man and you'll get there! How do I read the parable of the rich man and Lazarus? I don't read it as a reconnaissance report on hell—a hell I'm certain I'll never see because once-upon-a-time I prayed a salvation prayer. This parable is not a voyeur's view of the damned to inform the comfortable and curious. I have to read the parable as a rich man living in a world where at least a billion people long for the crumbs from my table. I don't read it and then think, "Well, after all, I prayed a sinner's prayer years ago so I don't need to worry about any of this." That would be to mock Jesus. The very thing the Pharisees did! To be a Christian means I am deliberately attempting to follow Jesus. Being a Christian does *not* mean I can ignore Lazarus with impunity! Being a Christian means I can no longer pretend that I don't see Lazarus laying at my door.

Lord Jesus, help us to heed your warnings; help us to see the Lazarus who lies at our door; help us to share the crumbs of our table. Amen.

DAY 17

mar 13

FRIDAY

Luke 18:9–14

Jesus Gives the Parable of the Pharisee and the Tax Collector

Most of us are predisposed to divide the world into good and bad people, the righteous and the unrighteous. But Jesus rarely does this. For Jesus the most dominant categories are the proud and the humble. We're all sinners. The question is, are we proud sinners or humble sinners? If we're proud sinners we concoct ways to justify ourselves in our own eyes by favorably comparing ourselves to those whom we deem worse than us. But if we are humble sinners we throw ourselves entirely on the mercy of God. This is what

Jesus sets forth in his parable of the Pharisee and the Tax Collector.

The Pharisees are a tragic story and a cautionary tale. The Pharisees weren't clerics like priests or Levites, rather the Pharisees were a religious-political party that arose around 150 years before the birth of Jesus. The Pharisees sought to preserve covenant fidelity during a time of forced Hellenization. The Pharisees urged their fellow Jews to preserve their Jewish identity and remain separate—Pharisee means separate—from the corrupting influence of the idolatrous pagan world. In its origin the Pharisee movement was squarely within the Hebrew prophetic tradition. We might think of Daniel and his three friends as examples of the original way to live as Pharisees within a Gentile empire. (The book of Daniel was written around the same time as the rise of the Pharisee movement.) The Pharisees were saying to their fellow Jews, "We are a covenant people and we need to maintain our allegiance to the God of Israel by remaining separate from the sins of idolatry." It's important to understand that the Pharisees began as a sincere and commendable movement seeking to preserve Jewish identity in a pagan ocean.

Unfortunately by the time of Jesus the Pharisees had devolved into the self-appointed morality police, deeply infected with a poisonous self-righteousness. They had become a sanctimonious "Take Back Israel for God" movement convinced of their own purity while aiming their censorious ire at "sinners"—sinners who were epitomized by the tax collectors. In *Wuthering Heights,* Emily Brontë captures what the Pharisees had become in this scathing sentence: "He was, and is yet most likely, the wearisomest self-righteous Pharisee who ever ransacked a Bible to rake the promises to himself and fling the curses to his neighbours." This is what can happen if we adhere to the seductive adage, "Hate the sin, but love the sinner." It sounds good, but almost always leads to the tragedy of the Pharisees. Jesus' parable of the Pharisee and the Tax Collector teaches us to love the sinner and hate our own sin.

In the Temple the Pharisee is fully aware of the tax collector as he vainly poses before God. The tax collector, on the other hand, is aware only of his own sin and his desperate need for God's mercy. And the tax collector is the only one who received God's mercy.

Today let's try to employ the ancient Christian practice of repeatedly praying the Jesus Prayer.

Lord Jesus Christ, Son of God, have mercy on me, a sinner. Amen.

DAY 18

Mar 14

SATURDAY

Luke 19:1–10

Jesus and Zacchaeus

Yesterday we looked at the Pharisees. But who were their despised foil, the tax collectors? Tax collectors were Jewish collaborators with the Roman occupiers. For a handsome profit they undertook the onerous task of collecting tax revenue for the Roman empire from their fellow Jews. Generally they employed no small amount of extortion and dishonesty in their work. They were both Benedict Arnold and Bernie Madoff. It's little wonder that though rich, they were generally despised, especially by the poor and pious. It's also significant to understand that the term "sinners" in the Gospels is not referring merely to those who sin, but to those who had been formally excluded from Jewish religious life because of particular sins, and at the top of that list were the colluding, cheating tax collectors. They were the ultimate *persona non grata* in Jewish life. The tax collectors were also the ultimate example of Jesus' controversial table practice of radical hospitality. Understanding who the tax collectors were helps us more clearly understand what's going on when Luke tells us, "The tax collectors and sinners were all drawing near to hear Jesus. And the Pharisees and the scribes grumbled, saying, 'This man receives sinners and eats with them.'" The scandal was that Jesus was willing to dine with excluded tax collectors and expelled sinners *before* they repented.

Jesus dined with both Pharisees and tax collectors. Jesus was willing to share a table with tax collectors despite their sins of dishonesty and extortion, and Jesus was willing to share a table with Pharisees despite their sins of self-righteousness and pride. When Jesus came to Jericho he dined with Zacchaeus, the chief tax collector. Jesus didn't require Zacchaeus to repent before sitting at table with him, and it doesn't appear that Jesus preached to Zacchaeus at the table. But before the meal was over Zacchaeus had pledged to amend his ways, right his wrongs, and give half his wealth to the poor. Such is the transformative power of the unconditional love that animated the ministry of

Jesus! What a thousand sermons from a hundred Pharisees could never accomplish, Jesus accomplished by simply sharing a meal with the most despised man in town.

Jesus then commented on Zacchaeus' repentance by saying, "Today salvation has come to this house." Salvation didn't come to Zacchaeus by inviting Jesus into his heart in some abstract way, but by actually inviting Jesus into his real life as it was, and suddenly discovering that because of Jesus he wanted to change his life. Salvation is not a mere change in our status, but a real transformation of our lives. Jesus brought salvation to a tax collector by simply alerting him to his true identity. At his core Zacchaeus wasn't really a con and a cheat; that was a corruption of his true identity. Zacchaeus was really a wayward son of Abraham who needed to be sought out in love and restored to the table of fellowship. Zacchaeus was a real life prodigal son redeemed by love.

Lord Jesus, may we again receive you into our lives so that your love and grace can save us by transforming us into true sons and daughters of God. Amen.

Day 19
Sunday

Luke 13:1–5

Jesus Warns Jerusalem

One of the themes of Jesus' prophetic ministry that becomes more and more prominent the closer he gets to Jerusalem is his dire warning about the impending fate of Jerusalem. In our Gospel reading for today, Jesus is informed about some Galilean pilgrims who were probably involved in a political uprising against the Roman occupation and were subsequently put to death by Roman soldiers in the Temple complex—thus mingling their blood with the sacrifices. Jesus' response is to tell them not to imagine that these Galilean victims were worse sinners than any other Galileans. Instead, Jesus says if they don't rethink their intentions they will all perish in the same way. Jesus then brings up an incident of a recent building collapse in Jerusalem that had resulted in eighteen fatalities and comments on it by saying, "Do you think that they were more blameworthy than all the others living in Jerusalem? No, I tell you! Unless you repent, you will all be destroyed in the same way."

What is Jesus saying? Is he talking about Galileans and Judeans going to hell? Yes and no. Jesus isn't talking about a postmortem spiritual hell, but an impending literal hell. Jesus has been calling Jerusalem into the kingdom of God and the way of peace by the practice of enemy love and radical forgiveness. But for the most part Jerusalem has rejected this message of peace, believing instead that when the time comes God will fight with them in a war of independence and help them attain freedom by killing their enemies. In response to this enormously dangerous holy war assumption, Jesus warns Jerusalem against resorting to violence by telling them that if they don't rethink war and peace according to the kingdom of God, they're all going to die by Roman swords and collapsing buildings.

And this is exactly what happened a generation later. After four years of violent revolution led by a cadre of false messiahs claiming that God was about to give Israel victory over Rome, General Titus and the

Roman Tenth Legion marched on Jerusalem. On August 4, AD 70, after a brutal four-month siege, the Romans launched their final assault. Hell had come to the holy city. Buildings collapsed from the bombardment of catapult stones (the hundred-pound hailstones of the Apocalypse), the city was set ablaze, and hundreds of thousands of Jerusalem's citizens were killed by Roman swords. In the end Jerusalem was reduced to a smoldering Gehenna—the garbage dump where the fires are never quenched and the maggots never die. This was when Jerusalem went to hell.

In the 21st century, the devil still tells big lies. In an age of nuclear, chemical, and biological weapons capable of eradicating all human life, the way of war is still foolishly romanticized and deemed a legitimate way to shape the world. But Lent is a time to repent, to rethink, to reimagine. Today let us heed the warning of Jesus and remember that there is no way to peace...peace *is* the way.

Lord Jesus, save us from our diabolical fascination with the ways of war. Help us by the Holy Spirit to imagine creative ways to wage peace. Amen.

DAY 20
MONDAY

John 8:1–11
Jesus and the Woman
Caught in Adultery

Today in our Lenten journey we move to the Gospel of John where we begin with one of the most beautiful and beloved stories in the Bible—the story of Jesus defending and forgiving the woman caught in adultery. Part of what is going on in this story is an attempt by the Pharisees to trap Jesus. The Pharisees weaponized the Bible in order to put Jesus in an impossible situation. According to Leviticus, adultery is indeed punishable by death. So the Pharisees accuse a woman of adultery, quote the Bible, and then demand a response from Jesus. If Jesus simply repudiates the Bible, the Pharisees will accuse Jesus of blasphemy—

another crime punishable by death in the Torah. But if Jesus sanctions an execution, he repudiates his own teaching. What Jesus does is sheer genius.

In the Old Testament (and in many other archaic societies), stoning was the means of communion execution. Why stoning? It's not the most efficient way to execute a human being, but stoning does have one important distinction over other means of execution: it can be carried out as a communal activity. Stoning allows everyone in the community to participate by throwing a stone, while allowing each individual to exonerate their own self by saying, "I didn't kill them; I only threw a stone." Of course Jesus is going to challenge this form of collective killing.

When the would-be executioners cited Moses and the sanction of stoning, Jesus refused to allow the Pharisees to act as a mob. People will do things as a mob they would never do as individuals. This is why angry mobs are quite literally the most dangerous human phenomenon. Søren Kierkegaard said, "The crowd is untruth." We can also say the mob is the satan. Jesus does not directly challenge the mob impulse, but forces each person to act as an individual. Jesus doesn't directly denounce the primitive practice of stoning a scapegoat, but instead calls each of them to engage in a moment of self-reflection, and then to act as responsible individuals. Jesus exorcises the mob spirit by saying, "Let the *one* among you all who is without sin cast the *first* stone." And with that brilliant sentence the demonic spell was broken. They could no longer act in satanic unison, but had to act as self-reflective individuals responsible for their own actions. When the community (no longer a mob) heard what Jesus had said, they went away *one by one*, beginning with the *elders*. Why were the elders the first to be delivered from the demonic mob spirit? Because, in general, elders are a bit closer to con-templative consciousness, the very thing necessary to break a mob spirit.

This story should speak to modern people in a particular way. Social media is especially susceptible to a mob spirit, and we must resist it. Let Lent be a time for us to repent of casting stones with the mob. Those of us who follow Jesus can never follow the crowd and must never act according to the mob spirit.

Lord Jesus, we thank you for your abundant forgiveness. Help us to go and sin no more by never

again joining the crowd intent on stoning the accused.
Amen.

DAY 21
TUESDAY

John 9:1–41
Jesus Heals the Man Born Blind

John constructs his Gospel around seven signs: the water turned to wine at Cana, the healing of the royal official's son in Capernaum, the healing of the lame man at the pool of Bethesda, the feeding of the five thousand at the Sea of Galilee, Jesus walking on water, the healing of the man born blind, and the raising of Lazarus from the dead. (And then there is the surprise eighth sign of Jesus' resurrection that marks the beginning of a new creation.) John doesn't talk about miracles, but signs. These signs are intended to point us to something significant about Jesus and his ministry.

The sixth sign of the healing of the man born blind takes up an entire chapter and is filled with drama as the man who was healed bests the Pharisees in theological debate and is expelled from the synagogue for it. The story opens with the disciples observing the man born blind and raising a theological question of who is to blame for it. But Jesus dismisses this line of questioning. Jesus is saying that when we observe suffering, the question isn't who is to blame, but how can we help. We've all seen Christian leaders assign blame upon the victims of epidemics, earthquakes, and tsunamis. But blame is what the satan does. Followers of Jesus are called to co-suffering love, not theological stone throwing. So Jesus instructs his disciples that when we observe suffering, it's not an opportunity to assign blame, but an opportunity to do the works of God by helping to heal, restore, and alleviate suffering. Blame is the devil's game—love is the high calling of the Christian. As Hans Urs von Balthasar said, "Love alone is credible; nothing else can be believed, and nothing else ought to be believed." And this brings us to the main point of the sixth sign.

The meaning of the sign is made explicit at the end of the story. Look at the last verse of the chapter as

Jesus says to the Pharisees, "If you were blind, you would not have sin, but now that you say, 'We see,' your sin remains." There is an innocence in admitting that we are too blind to pass judgment on others. We don't have to have an opinion on everything, especially when the question is who is to blame. It's enough for us to say, "I don't know who is to blame, I'm just here to help." But when we claim to have 20/20 vision in judging the sins of others and assigning blame, our own sin remains. This is the sin of Job's friends. They couldn't resist the temptation of trying to explain what had happened by blaming Job. The book of Job is a study in the seductive cruelty of blaming the victim. The lesson we should learn from the story of Jesus healing the man born blind and the Pharisees' reaction to it is that we should acknowledge our own blindness and let Jesus be both healer and judge.

Lord Jesus, we confess that we are too blind to pass judgment on others, so we turn away from seeking to blame and turn toward trying to love. Help us, we pray. Amen.

Day 22

Wednesday

John 10:1–21

Jesus and the Good Shepherd

In our Gospel reading today we see Jesus as the Good Shepherd who lays down his life for the sheep and brings abundant life. But who are the false shepherds—the thieves who come only to steal, kill, and destroy? To answer this we need to understand that the shepherd motif is messianic. The most common title for the Messiah was the Son of David, thus indicating that the Messiah would be a king, not only descended from David, but in someway *like* David—the shepherd who became king of Israel. At the end of Psalm 78, Asaph says that God took David from the sheepfolds and raised him up to shepherd Israel. And the prophet Micah famously predicted that the Messiah would be born in

Bethlehem, as David was, and that he would lead, feed, and protect the Lord's flock. By the time of Jesus, the Good Shepherd was an established metaphor for the Messiah. Thus the hirelings, the thieves, the bad shepherds in Jesus' teaching are the self-anointed false messiahs who were common throughout the first century.

We actually know quite a bit about theses false messiahs who rose and fell in and around the time of Jesus. There was Judas bar Hezekiah, a messiah who supported his movement through a band of highway robbers. Another would-be messiah was Athonges the Shepherd, a revolutionary who waged a guerilla war, killing Roman soldiers and Herodians, but in the end fled from the battlefield while his followers were being killed. Simon of Peraea was an escaped slave with messianic claims who destroyed Herod's palace in Jericho. So Jesus' description of these and other false messiahs is pointedly accurate—they came only to steal, kill, and destroy.

Jesus contrasts his messianic mission with the bad shepherds and false messiahs. He doesn't come to steal, but to serve the flock. He doesn't come to kill, but to lay down his life for the sheep. He doesn't come to destroy, but to bring abundant life. And in this passage Jesus hints that his flock will not be limited to the lost sheep of Israel when he says, "I have other sheep that do not belong to this fold. I must bring them in also, and they will listen to my voice. So there will be one flock, one shepherd."

Today let's listen for the peaceable voice of our Good Shepherd. We live in a time when there is an increase of demagogues and populist leaders making messiah-like claims—"Only I can fix it." But if it's a voice that cherishes the memory of colonialism (stealing), or endorses war because God is on our side (killing), or incites hostility toward vilified scapegoats (destruction), you can be sure it's not a voice that comes from the Good Shepherd, and is not a voice Christians should follow. Let us be so accustomed to listening to the voice of the unvarnished Jesus found in the Gospels that we are sheep who will not follow the voice of a stranger.

Lord Jesus, you are the Good Shepherd who leads us in the way of peace; help us to know your voice so well that we will never be taken in by the pretentions of false shepherds.

DAY 23
THURSDAY

John 11:1–44
Jesus Raises Lazarus

Our reading today is about Jesus greatest miracle. The raising of Lazarus is the climactic seventh sign in John's exquisitely crafted Gospel. John first introduces us to the ministry of Jesus with the whimsical sign of turning water to wine. This sign points us to Jesus as the one who brings the feast of the kingdom of God. John concludes his record of the ministry of Jesus, before moving into his Passion narrative, with Jesus' seventh and greatest sign—the raising of a man who was four days dead. This last sign points us to Jesus as the one who saves us from all that would destroy us, including our ultimate enemy, death itself.

Fyodor Dostoevsky was a genius at weaving gospel themes into his masterpieces. In his novel *Crime and Punishment* (which could be better translated as *Sin and Consequences*), the central character is an intelligent and impoverished student in St. Petersburg named Raskolnikov. In an effort to prove that he is a "great man" and thus "beyond good and evil" like Napoleon, Raskolnikov murders a pawnbroker and her sister. In the course of the story Raskolnikov befriends Sonya, a prostitute redeemed by Christ. In one of the most riveting scenes in the novel, Raskolnikov, who is about to confess his crime to Sonya, asks her to read to him the story of Jesus raising Lazarus. Before Sonya reads it, Raskolnikov asks her if she believes the story, to which she replies, "Yes, with all my heart." Of course, Raskolnikov is actually asking is there any hope for someone like him. Sonya then reads the story, but Dostoevsky doesn't just allude to it but quotes the entire story in his novel. The scene ends like this:

> "That's all about the raising of Lazarus," she whispered. The candle was flickering out in the battered candlestick, casting a dim light in this destitute room upon the murderer and

the harlot strangely come together over
the reading of the Eternal Book.

The raising of Lazarus is given to us as a sign conveying that no one is beyond the saving reach of Jesus Christ. No matter how dead we are in our sins, Jesus is the one who has the power to recall us back to life.

The seventh sign wrought upon Lazarus is also a foreshadowing of the Easter triumph. Jesus will defeat death because, as he told Martha, "I am the resurrection and the life." Or as the Orthodox Paschal Hymn says,

Christ is risen from the dead
Trampling down death by death
And upon those in the tombs
Bestowing life.

Lord Jesus, we believe that you are the Resurrection and the Life. Show us the glory of God by calling us out of our tombs of sin and restoring us to life. Amen.

DAY 24
FRIDAY

Mark 14:32–42
First Station of the Cross:
Jesus in Gethsemane

Today we begin the fourteen Scriptural Stations of the Cross—an adaptation of the traditional stations of the cross reflecting more deeply on the scriptural account of Christ's passion. (Pope John Paul II first celebrated the Scriptural Stations of the Cross on Good Friday, 1991.) In the stations of the cross we move ever deeper with Jesus into his Paschal passion—a trail of suffering that spans approximately eighteen hours, from his midnight arrest on Maunday Thursday to his burial at sunset on Good Friday. With the first station located in the garden of Gethsemane and the final station located in the garden of Joseph of Arimathea, the passion of Christ begins and ends in a garden, just as the story of the Bible begins in the garden of Eden and ends in the garden city of the New Jerusalem. The story of salvation really is the story of garden lost and garden regained.

Our meditations on the Man of Sorrows begin as we see the humanity of Jesus pressed to the breaking point in Gethsemane—an Aramaic word that means oil press. It's here in the garden of the oil press that the anointed Messiah is under such pressure that he says, "My soul is overwhelmed with sorrow to the point of death." This kind of language from Jesus shocks us. In Gethsemane we don't encounter a Jesus who is unflappable and impassible, but a Jesus who knows what it is to be under horrible pressure. At Gethsemane we don't see a Socrates cavalierly drinking the cup of hemlock, but a Jesus who three times pleads for the cup of death to be taken away from him. In Gethsemane we see the two natures of Christ in one person—first a human nature pleading, "remove this cup from me," but then a divine nature adding, "yet not what I will, but what you will."

To read the Gospels with unflinching honesty prevents us from sliding unwittingly into the ancient

Gnostic heresy of Docetism. Docetism (from the Greek word *dokein*, "to seem") denies the full humanity of Christ, claiming that Christ only *seemed* to be fully human. Too many modern Christians are de facto Docetists—they confess the full deity of Christ but have a hard time believing that Jesus was also fully human. The modern Docetist thinks of Jesus as God pretending to be human or God masquerading in human disguise. But at Gethsemane we see the full humanity of Christ on display as he recoils from suffering and death. At Gethsemane we are reminded that the Jesus who walked on water also sat at the well of Sychar weary from walking.

At Gethsemane we witness in hushed reverence as Jesus willingly empties himself of divine privilege in order to fully share in human suffering. The Apostle Paul describes the act of kenotic love like this: "Though he was God, he did not think of equality with God as something to cling to, but emptied himself." It is the willing descent of Christ into suffering and death that becomes the source of our salvation, or as the Apostle Peter says, "By his wounds we are healed."

Lord Jesus, as we see you in the garden of Gethsemane, willing to drink the cup of suffering down to the dregs of death, we thank you for redeeming our humanity by sharing our humanity. Amen.

DAY 25
SATURDAY

Mark 14:43–46

Second Station of the Cross:
Jesus Is Betrayed and Arrested

We all know that Jesus was betrayed by a kiss. But why did Judas do it? Why did he betray Jesus? Was it for the money? It's true Judas was a thief—the treasurer who was also an embezzler. Nevertheless, Judas was more complicated than a petty thief who betrays his rabbi for thirty coins. Judas' story gets complicated when he betrays Jesus *with a kiss*. Why the kiss? Why this theatrical embellishment? If Judas is betraying Jesus for money, why not just point him out— *that's the guy!*—take the money and run? If we can answer this question, I think we'll find that we don't have a simple story of a petty thief but a complicated tragedy, and a story that may leave us rather uncomfortable.

What do we know about Judas Iscariot? We know he was a disciple of Jesus. He was chosen by Christ to be one of his Apostles. Judas was to be among the select twelve leading a reimagined twelve tribes of Israel by announcing and enacting the kingdom of God. We know Jesus was aware that Judas would eventually betray him. We also have reason to suspect that prior to his becoming a disciple of Jesus, Judas belonged to a violent insurgency known as the Sicarii. Is Judas Iscariot, Judas the Sicarii-ite? Some scholars think so. The Sicarii ("dagger-men") were the most extreme faction of the Zealots—an insurgency advocating violent overthrow of the Roman occupation.

In the end it may not matter whether or not Judas belonged to the Sicarii. Judas and the rest of the disciples were undeniably locked into a paradigm of a violent Messiah. The Jewish understanding of Messiah's vocation included rescuing Israel from foreign oppressors and eventually ruling over the Gentiles. It was assumed this would be accomplished through the same kind violent means employed by the messianic prototypes of Joshua, David, and Judah Maccabaeus. So despite his message of loving enemies, turning the other cheek, and forgoing violent resistance to evil, the disciples were convinced that Jesus would eventually resort to violence. Eventually Jesus would alter his message, start killing Romans, and liberate Israel. Eventually Jesus would become *practical* and employ violence.

Was Judas trying to force Jesus to resort to violence and start the war for Jewish independence? I think so. The reason Judas greeted Jesus with the customary kiss (which was also a covert sign) is that Judas didn't so much want to *betray* Jesus as he wanted to *manipulate* Jesus. Judas wanted to provoke Jesus into launching a violent revolution. Judas wanted to remain a part of the inner circle of disciples following a now violent Jesus. Judas *acted* like he was still a faithful disciple because Judas wanted to *be* a faithful disciple— but only on his own terms. Judas didn't want to betray Jesus, he wanted to control Jesus. Judas wanted Jesus to be Messiah in a certain way—violent. When we try to make Jesus be the kind of king who will support our political agenda through violent power, we betray Jesus with a kiss.

Lord Jesus, may we be disciples who are faithful to you as you are, and never betray you with a kiss by trying to force you to be something other than you are. Amen.

DAY 26
SUNDAY

Luke 15:11–32
Jesus Gives the Parable of the
Prodigal Son

In 1669, the great Dutch painter Rembrandt turned this parable into one of his masterpieces—*The Return of the Prodigal Son.* Today this painting hangs in the Hermitage Museum in St. Petersburg, Russia where I have seen it more than once. It always brings tears to my eyes. There's a reason why Henri Nouwen once sat in front of the painting for eight hours.

In Rembrandt's *Return of the Prodigal* the reckless son has returned home from the far country. This boy has been to hell and you can tell. He's clothed in dirty and torn rags, in stark contrast to the luxurious robes of his father. He has the shaved head of a prisoner and his shoes have nearly disintegrated. The boy is kneeling in humility with his face buried in his father's chest. Rembrandt has worked with color and light in a way that draws our attention to the hands of the father as they rest tenderly upon his son. Strangely, the right hand is feminine and the left hand is masculine. Of course this is not due to some deficiency in the skill of the painter. Rembrandt seems to want to capture both the fatherly and motherly nature of God's love. This masterpiece is a portrait of a sinner in the hands of a loving God. Those of us who know the story realize that those hands will soon present his son with a rich robe, new shoes, and a costly ring. Then those hands will clap with authority as the father orders the preparation of a great feast to celebrate the return of his long lost son. This parable brims with theological significance as Jesus shows us that the heart of the Father contains no wrath toward sinners, but overflows with gratuitous love.

And what we *don't* find in the parable is just as significant. There is no appeasement theology. The father doesn't first rush to the servants' quarters to beat a whipping boy and satisfy his wrath before he can forgive his wayward son. No! In the story of the prodigal son, the father bears the loss and forgives his son from his treasury of inexhaustible love. He just forgives. There is no payment, no appeasement. Justice as *punishment* is what the resentful brother called justice. Justice as *reconciliation* is what the loving father called justice. The only wrath we find in the parable belongs to the Pharisee-like older brother, not the God-like father.

The ritual sacrifice of a substitute victim has nothing to do with the justice of God. As René Girard has shown, ritual sacrifice has its dark origins in the scapegoat mechanism where the tribe extinguishes the danger of all-against-all violence by killing a single victim. Ritual sacrifice does not originate in the heart of God, it originates in the violent heart of humanity. God does not require anyone to be killed in order to forgive! The fatted calf is killed, not to satisfy justice, but to provide the meal of reconciliation. Today I invite you to adapt your atonement theology to what Jesus teaches in his beautiful parable of forgiveness.

Lord Jesus, help us to see the beauty in the gospel of forgiveness as you have proclaimed it, and liberate us from our wrong ideas about an angry, violent, and retributive God. Amen.

Day 27
Monday

Matthew 26:57–68

Third Station of the Cross:

Jesus Before the Sanhedrin

After his arrest in the garden of Gethsemane by
the temple police, Jesus is brought to the high priest
Caiaphas for a late night trial before the Sanhedrin—the
religious ruling council of Jerusalem. After a series of
false witnesses fail to gain any corroboration, at last two
witnesses connect Jesus with something about the
impending destruction of the temple. When Jesus
remained silent before his accusers, the high priest in
frustration placed Jesus under oath and demanded to
know if he was the Messiah. Jesus responded
cryptically, saying, "You have said so," but then said

something truly astounding: "But I tell you, from now on you will see the Son of Man seated at the right hand of Power and coming on the clouds of heaven." With this the high priest tore his robes and screamed, "Blasphemy!" What is going on here? What is Jesus saying in claiming to be the mysterious Son of Man and why did it evoke such a volatile reaction from Caiaphas?

The "Son of Man" as an eschatological or "end times" figure originated in the apocalyptic book of Daniel and was enormously influential for how Jesus understood what he was doing. Jesus referred to the Son of Man no less than eighty times. In chapter seven of the book, Daniel dreams of a series of beasts coming up from the sea and wreaking havoc on earth. The first beast was like a lion, the second like a bear, the third like a leopard, the fourth a monstrous creature. These beasts represent the succession of arrogant empires throughout history that use military might to shape the world according to their own selfish agenda and fill the world with suffering. (These beasts are generally associated with the historic empires of Babylon, Persia, Greece, and Rome.) But then, as is typical in dreams, the perspective suddenly changes and Daniel finds himself a spectator in the court of heaven. God, as the Ancient of Days, is presiding and is ready to issue a judgment on behalf of a world oppressed by these beastly empires.

A human being (not a beast) called the Son of Man *ascends* from the earth into the clouds of heaven to stand before the Ancient of Days. This Son of Man is given dominion over all peoples, nations, and languages. The court of heaven announces that the kingdom of the Son of Man will never pass away or be destroyed. It was the hopeful vision that someday a human being would ascend from earth to heaven, be seated at the right hand of the Ancient of Days, and given dominion over the nations. It was in this way that humanity would be liberated from the oppression of an endless parade of beastly empires.

In his trial before the Sanhedrin, Jesus claims to be that Son of Man and tells Caiaphas that *from now on* you will see the Son of Man seated at the right hand of the Power. In other words, the endless age of the reign of Christ began two thousand years ago! Amen.

Lord Jesus, you are the Son of Man who has been given all power and dominion over the nations by the Ancient of Days. May we live as faithful subjects of the peaceable empire you have inaugurated. Amen.

Day 28

Tuesday

Matthew 26:69–75

Fourth Station of the Cross:

Jesus Is Denied by Peter

The ever-impetuous Peter had made a rash vow that he would never desert or deny Jesus, even if it meant prison or death. And in the garden of Gethsemane Peter had bravely drawn his sword and used it in defense of his master. But when Jesus disarmed Peter and healed the wounded man in the arresting party, all the fight went out of the brash fisherman. If Jesus wasn't going to fight for himself, why should he risk his life? So Peter fled from the garden. But later Peter secretly followed Jesus all the way into the courtyard of the high priest to see what would happen. And that's where things began to fall apart. Perhaps without even knowing what he was doing, Peter denied having any association with Jesus to a servant girl. Later he did it again. And when a group of bystanders said they didn't believe his denials because his country bumpkin Galilean accent gave him away, Peter cursed and swore he didn't know the man! That's when the rooster crowed. Matthew tells us what happened next in a short, painful sentence. "And he went out and wept bitterly."

I suppose we've all heard that rooster crow—the rooster of conviction that alerts us to how we've failed to live up to our lofty promise to faithfully follow Jesus. And we've all known the bitter tears of self-reproach induced by our failure. Yet this is one of the things I love about the Bible: it makes no attempt to cover up the sins of its seminal figures. We know about the crimes of Moses and David; we know about the failures of Abraham and Elijah; we know about the sins of Peter and Paul. Yet Moses and David, Abraham and Elijah, Peter and Paul are still presented as heroes of the faith. In the Bible all the saints are sinners.

And we who are sinners called to be saints should find comfort in this. It's not sin that disqualifies us as disciples of Jesus, but quitting. Peter denied Jesus, but he didn't quit, and he was forgiven and restored. Judas betrayed Jesus...and hung himself. Judas' betrayal of Jesus and Peter's denial of Jesus were not categorically different sins; they may have differed in culpability, but they were similar. If Peter could be forgiven and restored, so could Judas.

When you hear the rooster crow, you may weep bitterly for a while, but don't give up, don't quit, don't hang yourself. The rooster's crow of conviction doesn't signal the end of your journey, it just helps you get back on track. Just as Jesus restored Peter, Jesus can restore you. And it's from a place of restoration in our brokenness that we can actually help other people. This is exactly what Jesus told Peter: "I have prayed for you that your faith may not fail. And when you have turned back, strengthen your brothers." This is when we become what Carl Jung and Henri Nouwen described as "wounded healers."

Lord Jesus, we have all heard the rooster crow and shed our bitter tears because of our failures; forgive and restore us that we might help heal our brothers and sisters. Amen.

DAY 29

WEDNESDAY

Luke 23:13–25

Fifth Station of the Cross:
Jesus Is Condemned by Pilate

As the Roman governor Pontius Pilate—a man infamous in history for his cruelty—condemns Jesus to crucifixion, Barabbas is drawn into the sacred drama. Who was Barabbas? To understand the identity of Barabbas is to bring the tragedy of Good Friday into sharp focus—perhaps sharper than we would like. In understanding Barabbas, films like *The Passion of the Christ* have done us a disservice. Barabbas was not a deranged serial killer—why would a crowd ever clamor for the release of a common murderer? If we imagine Barabbas as a homicidal maniac, we will never imagine ourselves among the crowd shouting, "Give us Barabbas!" But we should.

Barabbas wasn't a common criminal, he was a national hero. Barabbas wasn't a serial killer, he was a political prisoner. Barabbas wasn't a murderous bandit, he was a revolutionary leader. Barabbas was a Jewish insurgent who had led an insurrection against the Roman occupation and who had killed someone during the uprising—probably a Roman soldier or a Jewish collaborator. Barabbas would have been viewed as a popular hero among much of Jerusalem's population who longed for liberation from foreign occupation by whatever means. Barabbas wasn't the Boston strangler. Barabbas was William Wallace or George Washington or Che Guevara. *That* casts Barabbas in a completely different light!

Some ancient New Testament manuscripts give us the revolutionary's full name as Jesus Barabbas, that is, Jesus Son of the Father. Jesus Barabbas is a rival messiah! On Good Friday we are given the choice between two versions of Jesus—Jesus Barabbas or Jesus of Nazareth. Jesus of Nazareth calls us to the way of peace by loving our enemies and the practice of radical forgiveness. Jesus Barabbas is willing to fight our wars and kill our enemies in the name of freedom.

Recently a well-known megachurch pastor said, "When I'm looking for a leader I want the meanest, toughest son of a gun I can find." Whether he understands it or not, this evangelical pastor is saying, "Give us Barabbas!" For many American Christians the politics of Jesus are dismissed as impractical and so they kick the can down the road saying, "maybe someday we can turn our swords into plowshares, but now is the time for us to build more B-2 bombers and stockpile nukes so we can kill all our enemies." The crowd that gathers on Good Friday shouting, "Give us Barabbas!," is far more plausible and numerous than most of us imagine. If we think that killing our enemies is compatible with Christian ethics, we are in effect saying, "Give us Barabbas!"

But Lent is the time to rethink everything in the light of Christ. We are not called to scrutinize the Sermon on the Mount through the lens of the Pentagon; we are called to follow Jesus by embodying the kingdom of God here and now, no matter what the rest of the world does.

Lord Jesus, forgive us for the times we have

unwittingly asked for Barabbas because we were still enchanted by the ways of violence; lead us in your ways of peace. Amen.

Day 30

Thursday

Mark 15:15–20

Sixth Station of the Cross:
Jesus Is Scourged and Mocked

Jesus came to Jerusalem to begin his reign. To be crowned King of the Jews in Jerusalem was the culmination of his mission to establish the kingdom of God. All of Jesus' followers understood this. If we had asked Jesus' disciples in the spring of AD 30 why they were going to Jerusalem at Passover, they would have said, "So that Jesus can become King and usher in the reign of God." And this is entirely correct. What the disciples *didn't* understand—even though Jesus had plainly told them—was *how* Messiah would become King. On Palm Sunday Jesus arrived in Jerusalem and the Galilean Passover pilgrims shouted, "Blessed is the King who comes in the name of the Lord." But Good Friday is his coronation day.

After Pilate had released the popular revolutionary, Barabbas, and condemned Jesus to crucifixion, Jesus was taken into the Antonia Fortress where the entire battalion of Roman soldiers staged a mock coronation of the man who had just been sentenced to death for claiming to be the King of the Jews. First they subjected him to the dreaded Roman flagellation—a gruesome scourging known as "the half death." Then the soldiers crowned him with thorns, donned him with a purple robe, saluted and bowed down to him, saying, "Hail, King of the Jews!" while spitting on him and beating him with the cane that served as his scepter. The scene is horrific.

The Roman soldiers did what they did to Jesus as a cruel mockery, nevertheless this is the true coronation of the world's true King, this is the royal pageant for the King of Kings. His acclaim is by insult, his crown is made of thorns, his scepter is a reed, the homage paid him is done in mockery, his procession is to carry his cross through town, and his throne will be that very cross. Yes, it's awful. But it's also paradoxically glorious, for this is how Jesus Christ became King of Kings. This is how God's Kingdom of Love entered into a cruel world energized by hate. Jesus will not become King at his Second Coming, Jesus became King on Good Friday.

Jesus became King on Good Friday in the same way his Kingdom still comes today. It comes by co-suffering love expressed in forgiveness. It doesn't come by the Machiavellian machinations of politics or by the blood letting of a battlefield. How the Kingdom of Christ comes into the world has nothing to do with who sits in the White House or with who runs the Pentagon. When we are mesmerized by these conventional means of power, thinking we need to possess them in order to change the world, it reveals that we still have not comprehended the Paschal mystery and have still not understood that Christ has no need for Caesar's sword. Let us no longer be enamored by the ways of Caesar, ancient and modern, for it has nothing to do with how the Kingdom of God comes.

Lord Jesus, in deep solemnity and in pure worship we bow before you and say, "Hail to the

King." Help us to believe that your Kingdom comes by love and only by love. Amen.

DAY 31
FRIDAY

John 19:16–17
7th Station of the Cross: Jesus Is Given His Cross

As Jesus carries his cross to Golgotha, we are reminded of this moment in Genesis:

> "Abraham took the wood of the burnt offering and laid it on his son Isaac."

Like Isaac carrying the wood of his own sacrifice to Mount Moriah, Jesus now carries the wood of his own sacrifice to Golgotha. But unlike Isaac, for Jesus there will be no reprieve from sacrifice. Why? Jesus had already explained this to the Jerusalem crowd.

In John 8, a group of Judeans in Jerusalem announce to Jesus that they believe he is the Messiah and are ready to become his disciples. Jesus responds by telling them that if they hold to his teaching they will become genuine disciples and the truth will set them free. The Judeans object to this by saying they are children of Abraham who are free and are slaves to no one. Jesus counters by telling them they are slaves of sin and children of the devil, and whether they know it or not they are ready to kill him. When the Judeans insist that Abraham is their father, Jesus replies, "If you were Abraham's children, you would be doing what Abraham did, but now you seek to kill me, a man who has told you the truth that I heard from God. This is not what Abraham did." From there it all goes downhill fast as they shout at Jesus saying, "you are a Samaritan and have a demon!" By the end of the chapter they are attempting to stone Jesus. So much for becoming disciples.

The key to understanding this sad episode of abandoned discipleship is when Jesus tells them, "If you were Abraham's children, you would be doing what Abraham did." What did Abraham do that these people in Jerusalem were not doing? Abraham put down the knife. In the crucial moment, Abraham realized that God does not require human sacrifice and he put down the knife. If Abraham is the father of monotheism, he is also the father of the abolition of human sacrifice. But the Judeans still believe that it's God's will for certain people to be put to death in God's name. This is why Jesus tells them they are of the devil—the father of lies who working through Cain "was a murderer from the beginning." Those who hold to the idea of human sacrifice through collective killing are following the devil, even if they try to tell themselves they believe in Jesus.

On Good Friday the way of Cain prevails among the crowd. Just as Cain killed Abel, now the crowd will kill Jesus. The crowd under the sway of the satan will again murder an innocent Abel. But the sacrifice of Jesus will tell the truth, expose the lie, and become the sacrifice to end sacrificing. And just as Isaac's story did not end at Moriah, so Jesus' story does not end at Golgotha.

Lord Jesus, help us to be like Abraham and put down the knife; help us to understand that no one ever again needs to be put to death in order to accomplish the will of God; help us to be the children of God who choose mercy over sacrifice. Amen.

Day 32

Saturday

Mark 15:21

Eighth Station of the Cross:
Simon of Cyrene Carries Jesus' Cross

Today's reading is only one verse, but it contains an enormous message—when Jesus came to the end of his strength, there was someone there to carry his cross for him. As Jesus faltered under the load of the cross, Simon of Cyrene was given the supreme honor of carrying it for him. Mark tell his readers that Simon, a Jewish Passover pilgrim from North Africa, is the father of Alexander and Rufus. Alexander and Rufus were bishops in the first century church, and so presumably Simon himself, the one who had carried Jesus' cross to Golgotha, became a believer. I like to think about

Simon of Cyrene worshipping in one of the first-century house churches and his fellow believers whispering to one another, "the cross-bearer is here." Can you imagine meeting the man who carried Jesus' cross?!

From the story of Simon of Cyrene we are reminded that there are limits to what we can bear, but when we reach those limits God will send someone to help. David was the great hero who had killed Goliath, but there was a giant David couldn't kill. When Ishbi-benob, the brother of Goliath, was about to kill David because the king had grown weary in battle, Abishai came to David's rescue and slew the giant. Elijah was the mighty man of God who called down fire from heaven and prevailed in his contest with the four hundred prophets of Baal. But when the prophet fled from Jezebel and was depressed, curled up in a fetal position under a broom tree praying to die, God arranged for Elisha to become his companion and to share his prophetic mantle. And when Jesus Christ the Son of God reached his limit and could carry his cross no more, there was Simon of Cyrene to carry it for him.

Some days we can slay Goliath with a slingshot, some days we can't. Some days we can call down fire from heaven, some days we're curled up under the broom tree. Some days we can handle anything, some days it's all too much. That's when we need someone to help us. There was a giant David couldn't kill, so Abishai did it for him. There was a trial Elijah couldn't handle, so Elisha was given to him. And there was a cross Jesus couldn't carry, but Simon of Cyrene was there to carry it for him.

This is the beauty of the body of Christ and why the church is so necessary. Christianity is not a solo project; we can't go it alone. David couldn't do it by himself. Elijah couldn't do it by himself. Even Jesus couldn't do it by himself. And you can't do it by yourself. Some days we have the honor of being Simon of Cyrene and helping a brother or sister carry their cross when it has become too much for them. Other days we are the one in need of a Simon of Cyrene. Whether we are helping or being helped, it's all the grace of God.

Lord Jesus, send us a Simon of Cyrene when we've reached our limit; and help us to be a Simon of Cyrene to those faltering around us. Amen.

DAY 33
SUNDAY

John 12:20–33
Jesus Talks About What His Death Will Accomplish

On three occasions in Galilee, Jesus foretold of his death by crucifixion. But in Jerusalem Jesus talked about the *meaning* of his death—and this is enormously significant for those who seek to interpret how the death of Jesus saves us.

Some Greeks who have come to Jerusalem for Passover ask Philip for an audience with Jesus. (Philip is the only disciple with a Greek name; he may have had a Greek father and was presumably fluent in Greek.) When Jesus learns of Greeks seeking him out, he seems unsurprised, knowing that his gospel would eventually expand beyond the Jewish world. But then Jesus speaks about this growth of the gospel occurring only after he has been buried in the ground as a seed. And Jesus doesn't speak of death nonchalantly, instead he indicates that his soul is deeply troubled by the approach of death. Yet Jesus cannot seek to escape death, because he understands that his death is inseparably linked to the entire purpose of his life. In this passage Jesus doesn't just speak of his death but speaks of being "lifted up"—a euphemism for crucifixion.

But what does the crucifixion of Jesus Christ accomplish? This is one of the few passages in the Gospels where Jesus offers any interpretative meaning to his death. He says his crucifixion will accomplish three things:

1. It will judge the world.
2. It will cast out the ruler of the world.
3. It will draw the whole world to him.

The cross of Christ pronounces judgment on the basic arrangement of the world. The principalities and powers—the rich and powerful, the structures they represent, and the spirit generated by them—claim they have the right to rule the world because they are wise and just. But the cross exposes the principalities and the powers as neither wise nor just, but simply greedy for wealth and power. The cross judges the system of the world as capable of unimaginable crimes.

The cross also drives out the ruler of this world—the satan. The satan (accuser) unites people around the practice of scapegoating a vilified other, but the cross exposes scapegoating for what it is—the lynching of an innocent victim. Where the satanic scapegoat mechanism is exposed, the satan is eventually cast out, and the cross is the ultimate exposé of scapegoating.

Finally, the cross re-founds the world. When we see Jesus lifted up on the cross, perfectly displaying the love of God by forgiving the sin of the world, we find the place where human society is reorganized. Instead of a world organized around an axis of power enforced by violence, we discover a world organized around an axis of love expressed in forgiveness. As we gaze long upon the sacred mystery of Christ crucified, we find ourselves being drawn into the saving orbit of love and forgiveness.

Lord Jesus, as we see you lifted up in crucifixion, may we be drawn into a new orbit around your cross as the axis of love expressed in forgiveness. Amen.

DAY 34

MONDAY

Luke 23:27–31

Ninth Station of the Cross:
Jesus and the Weeping Women

Not everyone in Jerusalem belonged to the crowd that shouted, "Crucify him!" Here we find women from Jerusalem weeping as the innocent Galilean prophet is led away to an unjust execution. Here we also see the unfathomable depth of Jesus' compassion as he weeps for those who weep for him—even as he is about to be crucified. But why does Jesus tell these compassionate women not to weep for him, but for themselves and their children? Because Jesus knows the horror that will befall Jerusalem within forty years. Jesus knows that Jerusalem will fall under the unspeakable cruelties of siege warfare; that disease and famine will ravage the populace; that civil war will breakout among the factions within the besieged city; that the Roman Tenth Legion will crucify so many people desperately trying to escape Jerusalem that the soldiers will run out of trees; that in the end most of Jerusalem's population will die by famine, pestilence, and sword; that those who do manage to survive the horrors of the siege will do so only to be enslaved by the Romans. Jesus tells the women of Jerusalem to weep for the agonies that await them and their children. These tender-hearted women wept over Jesus being condemned to crucifixion, but within a generation Jerusalem itself will be crucified.

Jesus had tried to pull Jerusalem back from its hell-bent ways, but he knew that he had only given Jerusalem a forty-year stay of sentence. Jesus was the green tree who taught and embodied the way of peace and love, yet he was still crucified. The sons of the weeping women of Jerusalem will be the dry wood who will foolishly advocate for the way of war. Jesus is saying that if the Romans can inflict such a fire of suffering on the green tree of peacemaking, what amount of suffering will they kindle in the dry trees of war-waging. Jesus weeps for these women and their children because he knows that Jerusalem is headed for hell—the hell of war.

To glamorize war is to pave the road to hell. To excitedly anticipate war is to rush headlong down the road to hell. To recklessly claim that God is on our side in waging war is to cause Jesus to weep for us. In his song, "With God on Our Side," Bob Dylan excoriates the folly of thinking that God is on our side in war, and the final verse tells the truth as only a poet-prophet can.

> So now as I'm leavin'
> I'm weary as Hell
> The confusion I'm feelin'
> Ain't no tongue can tell
> The words fill my head
> And fall to the floor
> If God is on our side
> He'll stop the next war

Lord Jesus, save us from the folly of thinking that war is something you can bless. Help us to see that with your crucifixion and resurrection war has been abolished, and the time has come for us to turn swords into plowshares. Amen.

Day 35
Tuesday

Luke 23:33–38

Tenth Station of the Cross:
Jesus Is Crucified

The Bible is an enormous and often unwieldy book. For the Christian, the Bible is our inspired and sacred text, and the primary (though not exclusive) source for the formation of our theology. But it is the height of naiveté to imagine that we can just "take the Bible as it is." The Bible as it is presents some daunting challenges—it has to be first translated and then interpreted, and the interpretive options are myriad. We can find biblical warrant for just about any position if we want to engage in the folly of proof-texting—and violence is the easiest thing to justify by proof-texting.

The practice of justifying violence by an unscrupulous use of the Bible has a sad and sordid history from crusaders to colonizers, from grand inquisitors to grand wizards.

What we need is to find a way to center our reading of the Bible; we need to find the interpretive center of our sacred text and read the rest of Scripture from that vantage point. Where do I center my reading of Scripture? For me it's as simple as locating the decisive moment in the great story the Bible tells. So it's in the New Testament; it's in the Gospels; it's in the words of Jesus; it's at the cross. My interpretive center of the Bible is found right here in today's Gospel reading: "Father, forgive them, for they know not what they do."

I read and interpret the entirety of Scripture from the lofty vantage point of Mount Calvary where Jesus hangs upon a cross with his arms outstretched in proffered embrace imploring forgiveness for his murderers. I don't center my reading of Scripture in the archaic laws of the Levitical code; I don't center my reading of Scripture in the wars of Joshua and David; I don't center my reading of Scripture in the dark violence of the Old Testament; I don't center my reading of Scripture in the enigmatic texts of Revelation. I center my reading of Scripture in Jesus' words of forgiveness spoken from the cross. Whether it's the violence of the Flood, the violence of the Exodus, the violence of the Conquest, or the violence of the Apocalypse, I interpret everything in the light of Good Friday when Jesus prays, "Father forgive them, for they know not what they do."

The Old Testament is the inspired telling of Israel's story of coming to know the living God, but inevitably assumptions are made along the way. The Bible does not stand above the story it tells, but is itself fully immersed in the story. The goal is to continue on the spiritual journey that the Bible documents until we reach the climactic moment of Good Friday. There is nothing more central to my understanding of God than this:

God is like Jesus.

God has always been like Jesus.

There's never been a time when God was not like Jesus.

We haven't always known this, but now we do.

Lord Jesus, when we look at you upon the cross forgiving your murderers, we discover the God who would rather die than kill his enemies. Help us to read the rest of Scripture in this holy light. Amen.

Day 36
Wednesday

Luke 23:39–43

Eleventh Station of the Cross:

Jesus and the Two Thieves

When we think of crucifixion we instinctively think of Jesus for obvious reasons. But this may cause us to think that crucifixion was something relatively unique to Jesus. It was not. The Roman Empire crucified hundreds of thousands of victims. Indeed, one of the scandals of Good Friday is that Jesus was but one of three that day. Jesus was not even granted the macabre dignity of his own crucifixion, but was among a trio of victims. Jesus doesn't die as a lone sufferer, but as Immanuel among the sufferers. It's here that the Man of Sorrows drinks the cup of suffering down to its bitter dregs.

On Good Friday we behold the gruesome spectacle of the God-Man nailed to a tree. This is the only theodicy that comes close to working. Yes, life is filled with horrible and undeserved suffering, but God does not exempt himself from it; rather God in Christ fully shares it with us. As God the suffering of Christ is wholly unique; but as a human his suffering is in solidarity with all human suffering. Golgotha is where divine impassability intersects with human suffering. Often human suffering seems pointless and meaningless, but it is a pointless meaninglessness shared by God and Christ. And once God is involved it is no longer pointless or meaningless...for by his wounds we are healed.

Christ crucified with victims on either side of him also presents us with a powerful image: Jesus among the victims in solidarity with them, but simultaneously becoming the dividing point. To see Jesus Christ hung upon a cross wearing a crown of thorns, with victims on either side, is, perhaps, the most powerful single image of the gospel. Incarnation, forgiveness, and kingdom are all present. The three crosses of Golgotha also presents us with the image of choice—for how we respond to Jesus determines everything.

One of the crucified revolutionaries sees in Jesus the possibility of a new kingdom and believes. This is a remarkable thing and one of the greatest expressions of faith to be found in all of Scripture. This victim sees the inscription, "Jesus of Nazareth, King of the Jews," and believes that Jesus truly is a king with a kingdom and asks to be remembered in this coming kingdom. To this dying man Jesus promises union with him in Paradise.

The other crucified revolutionary, though himself a victim, can't resist participating in the old way of victimizing others. This is the seductive power of scapegoating—even as he dies on a cross, this victim finds cruel solace in joining the crowd in blaming another. But when we deal with our fear and anger, our pain and shame by blaming others, we achieve union with the satan, and that keeps us locked in our own self-imposed hell. One thief sees in Jesus the possibility of a new kingdom centered in forgiveness and believes. The other thief cannot resist the old satanic way of exporting guilt through blame...but only one response leads to the Paradise of union with Christ.

Lord Jesus, we look to you on the cross wearing your crown of thorns and believe in your kingdom of love and forgiveness. Jesus, remember us and lead us into the blessed Paradise of union with you. Amen.

DAY 37
THURSDAY

John 19:25–27
Twelfth Station of the Cross:
Jesus Gives His Mother to John

At Golgotha we find a crowd of cruel mockers and jeering priests and they only add to the horrors of that long day's dying. But they aren't the only people there, for at the foot of the cross we also find family and friends of Jesus, and this provides us with one of the most tender moments of the Passion. Even as Jesus is dying on the cross, his love and compassion reaches out to others as he commits his mother and John to a relationship of mutual care: "Here is your son. Here is your mother." Looking down upon them from the cross, Jesus draws Mary and John into a new mother-son relationship: "And from that hour the disciple took her into his own home."

What we have in this episode with Jesus, Mary, and John is a poignant picture of Jesus' vision for his church—a community of faith centered around our Lord and his cross, caring for one another. We really should see the church as our mother; and the church really should think of its members as beloved children. I know the experience of church doesn't always live up to this vision, and I know it's easy to be critical of the church, but still I hear Jesus say, "Here is your mother." I have no quibble with the Orthodox and Catholic veneration of Mary, but I do prefer to see Mary as a revered personification of the church. So when I hear Jesus speaking from the cross directing a disciple to care for his mother, I take it as a sacred plea from Christ to care lovingly for the church as our mother.

And so my commitment to Jesus is in part expressed in a filial devotion to the church. Jesus is my Lord and Savior, but the church is my mother—a mother who both provides care and is to be cared for. I'm speaking of the church not as a cold (and sometime cruel) institution, but as the kind of community where many people have their only real opportunity to find love, acceptance, and dignity. As a pastor I know of many people where the church has truly become a mother to them. I know of situations where the church has treated specific people better than their own mother.

At its best there's nothing like the church. A place where Matthew 25 is just a normal day—a place where the poor are fed and clothed, the sick are helped and healed, a place where the immigrant is welcomed, and the prisoner is given dignity. A place where everyone is saint and sinner. A place where a judge and a felon can sit side by side on the same pew with equal status in Christ. A place where we not only carry each other's burdens, but when necessary carry each other, because, despite our vast differences in education and opportunity, opinions and politics, we are learning to love one another like Jesus loves us—unconditionally. This is the church I believe in.

Lord Jesus, help us to behold the church as our mother. And help us to care for our mother, the church, in such a way that she can provide motherly love and care for her sons and daughters. Amen.

DAY 38
FRIDAY

Mark 15:33–37 & Luke 23:44–46
Thirteenth Station of the Cross:
Jesus dies

In our journey through the Passion of Christ as set forth in the stations of the cross we have arrived at the death of Jesus, and truly we are treading upon holy ground. As Jesus neared his death he cried out, "My God, my God, why have you forsaken me?" What are we to make of the Cry of Dereliction? Was Jesus actually forsaken by God? Had God turned his back on his Son? Was there truly a rupture in the Trinity? The correct theological answer is a clear and unequivocal, No! But that is not to diminish the existential experience of God-forsakenness that Jesus Christ fully entered into—an experience that is common to all of us at one time or another.

The wrenching words, "My God, my God, why have you forsaken me?," are the opening lines of Psalm 22. This psalm—known as the Psalm of the Cross—can be read under this banner: Last Thoughts of a Dying Messiah. In this psalm we find numerous allusions to the crucifixion. Here are a few examples:

> All who see me laugh me to scorn;
> they curl their lips and wag their heads, saying,
> "He trusted in the LORD; let him deliver him;
> let him rescue him, if he delights in him."

> All of my bones are out of joint.
> my tongue sticks to the roof of my mouth;
> and you have laid me in the dust of the grave.

> They pierce my hands and feet;
> they divided my garments among them;
> they cast lots for my clothing.

This is the psalm that is in the mind of Jesus as he is dying. But the sense of God-forsakenness is not all there is in Psalm 22. Later we find lines like this:

For he did not ignore nor scorn
the suffering of the afflicted one;
he has not hidden his face from me,
but heard when I cried to him.

Jesus knows what it is to *feel* forsaken by God, and in his suffering Jesus uttered the bewildered Cry of Dereliction. But in his death Jesus committed his spirit into the hands of the Father he knows will never forsake him. Sometimes when we've done all we can do, there's nothing more to be done than to put everything in the hands of the God who will never abandon us.

Lord Jesus, we thank you that you have fully shared with us what it feels like to be utterly forsaken; but we thank you even more that you have promised that you will never leave nor forsake us. Amen.

DAY 39
SATURDAY

John 19:38–42
Fourteenth Station of the Cross:
Jesus Is Buried

Today we've come to the final station in our
contemplative journey through the fourteen Scriptural
Stations of the Cross. At the fourteenth station we find
not Christ in suffering, but Christ in death. Today we
see Jesus dead upon the cross. As we see a soldier
pierce his side and blood and water mysteriously flow,
we cannot help but think of the twin sacraments of
Baptism and Eucharist. Indeed, the church is brought
forth from the opened side of Christ. Even as from the
side of the first Adam placed in a deep sleep Eve was
brought forth, now from the riven side of the Last Adam

in the deeper sleep of death the bride of Christ is brought forth.

We watch in hushed reverence as Nicodemus and Joseph of Arimathea take the body of Jesus down from the cross, prepare it for burial, and lay it in the garden tomb. And it's with the setting of the sun on Good Friday and the arrival the Sabbath known to us has Holy Saturday that we can truly say, "God is dead." And is there any more jarring phrase than, "God is dead"?

Long before Friedrich Nietzsche used the phrase "God is dead" to describe the spiritual condition of late modernity, the early Lutherans used it in a Holy Saturday hymn.

> O darkest woe!
> Ye tears, forth flow!
> Has earth so sad a wonder?
> God the Father's only Son
> Now is buried yonder!
> O sorrow dread!
> Our God is dead!

There truly was a time when it could be said that God is dead, because whatever it means for a human being to experience the final dissolution of death, God in Christ has fully experienced. When we speak of Incarnation and Immanuel our minds are immediately drawn to Christmas and the babe wrapped in swaddling clothes lying in the manger. But Christ is never more Immanuel than when he is wrapped in grave clothes lying in the tomb. Yes, Jesus Christ is God with us in birth and life, but he is also God with us in sorrow and death.

There are two ways of looking at Holy Saturday. One is from the perspective of the living, where there is nothing to be done but to weep and wait, and indeed much of life is lived in the liminal space of Holy Saturday. But there is another perspective of Holy Saturday, and that is the perspective of Death itself. On Holy Saturday Jesus is not inactive, but has descended into Death to destroy Death by death. This is what the church fathers described as the harrowing (or distressing) of Hades. On Holy Saturday Death dared to swallow God, but Death cannot digest divinity. Death's brazen attempt to swallow Christ will lead to Death's demise. But now at the final station of the cross all we can do is wait for what comes next.

Lord Jesus, truly you are Immanuel, God with us in birth, life, sorrow, and death, that we might be with you in resurrection and everlasting life. Amen.

DAY 40
PALM SUNDAY

Luke 19:28–44
Jesus Makes His Triumphal Entry

Today is the first day of Holy Week—the journey from Palm Sunday to the end of Lent on Holy Saturday. More than any week in the year this is a time for deep reflection on the life and message of Jesus Christ.

Jesus' triumphal entry on Palm Sunday sets up a confrontation with the principalities and powers represented by King Herod, the high priest Caiaphas, and the Roman governor Pontius Pilate. The Roman governor ordinarily resided at a Herodian palace in the coastal city of Caesarea, but during Passover (a feast celebrating Jewish liberation from foreign domination) the governor had to be in Jerusalem to suppress any uprisings that might occur during this volatile week. Coming from Caesarea, Pilate entered the city from the west, riding a warhorse at the head of the Imperial Calvary. The Roman governor's entrance into Jerusalem was essentially a military parade. It was intended as a show of force to intimidate any would-be revolutionaries. Military parades, then and now, are how empires demonstrate that they rule the world through their superior capacity to wage war.

When Jesus arrived at the Mount of Olives east of Jerusalem, he deliberately enacted this five-hundred-year-old prophesy from Zechariah.

> Rejoice greatly, O daughter of Zion!
> Shout aloud, O daughter of Jerusalem!
> See, your king comes to you;
> triumphant and victorious is he,
> humble and riding on a donkey,
> on a colt, the foal of a donkey.
> He will take away the chariot from Ephraim,
> and the warhorse from Jerusalem.
> The weapons of war will be broken,
> and he will teach peace to the nations;
> his dominion shall be from sea to sea,
> and from the River to the ends of the earth.

Coming from the Mount of Olives, Jesus not only entered Jerusalem from the opposite direction than the Roman governor, but in the opposite *manner*. Instead of riding a warhorse like Pilate and all the warhorse riders throughout history, Jesus rides a donkey, and not even a full grown donkey, but a donkey's colt. Jesus' triumphal entry was the anti-military parade. It was a mockery of Rome's intimidating show of military power. It also presented Jerusalem with a stark contrast between the way of war and the way of peace. At the beginning of Holy Week, Pontius Pilate and Jesus of Nazareth are at the head of two very different parades. The question for us is which parade are we marching in—the military parade of Pilate that still believes the world is to be shaped by war, or the peace parade of Jesus that understands that with the coming of Christ war has been abolished?

Lord Jesus, on this Palm Sunday may our hosannas herald the arrival of the Prince of Peace and may we ever march in your parade of peace. Amen.

Day 41
Holy Monday

Mark 11:12–23
Jesus Disrupts the Temple

On Palm Sunday Jesus arrived in Jerusalem but did not spend the night in the city. It was far too dangerous to stay in Jerusalem at night when the temple police could arrest him without fear of a riot. So in the evening Jesus retreated to Bethany on the Mount of Olives and then returned to teach in the temple each morning. On Monday Jesus enacted two pieces of prophetic theater that are highly significant. As he walked down the Mount of Olives from Bethany on his way to the Temple, he stopped to look for fruit on a fig tree. This was a theatrical performance—obviously Jesus knew it wasn't the season for figs. Upon finding no fruit, he spoke to the fig tree, saying, "May no one ever eat fruit from you again." Then he continued his journey to the temple where he engaged in another fruit inspection, and failing to find the fruit of fidelity and justice—the fruit the Hebrew prophets always called Israel to bear—Jesus staged an even more dramatic performance of prophetic theater.

Jesus made a whip and drove out the sheep for the sacrifices, overturned the tables of the moneychangers and the seats of the pigeon sellers, and shouted, "My house shall be called a house of prayer for all nations, but you have made it a den of robbers!" Jesus is the climax of the Hebrew prophetic tradition. What is traditionally called the "cleansing of the temple" was not a cleansing at all, but a prophetic denunciation and a symbolic destruction of the temple. Six centuries earlier the prophet Jeremiah had denounced the temple as a den of robbers, meaning that the people of Jerusalem were using the temple as a hideout, believing that it gave them exemption from divine judgment for their idolatry and injustice. Jeremiah then predicted that the temple would be destroyed by fire that "will burn and not be quenched." This prophecy came to pass about twenty years later in

587 BC when Jerusalem and the temple were destroyed by the Babylonians.

On Holy Monday Jesus re-enacted Jeremiah's prophetic protest—a symbolic act that the priests, scribes, and Levites would have easily interpreted. Just as Jeremiah had predicted the destruction of the first temple, now Jesus is predicting the destruction of the second temple. Like the fig tree, the temple was barren of the fruit that God sought and it would never produce fruit again.

Jesus' action of temporarily halting the temple sacrifices during Passover week was highly provocative and extremely dangerous. It was only due to his popularity with the crowds of Passover pilgrims that Jesus wasn't arrested on Monday. Nevertheless this action accelerated the plot among the chief priests to find a way to arrest Jesus in secret and have him put to death. More than anything else it was his prophetic protest in the temple on Monday that sealed Jesus' fate. There's nothing hypocritical religion fears and hates more than bold prophetic action. This is religion at its worst.

Lord Jesus, you are the greatest of all the prophets; we ask that we may be given grace to hear and heed the prophetic word you would speak to us during these final days of Lent. Amen.

DAY 42
HOLY TUESDAY

Luke 21:5–33
Jesus Gives the Olivet Discourse

On Tuesday of Holy Week Jesus delivered his Olivet Discourse to his disciples, predicting that despite the impressive grandeur of Herod's temple, within a generation the temple would be destroyed with "not one stone left upon another." In the Olivet Discourse Jesus is not talking about the end of the world, but the end of the age—the end of the temple age. In John's Gospel, when Jesus stages his protest in the temple and the authorities demand a sign to justify his actions, Jesus says the sign will be this: "Destroy this temple and in three days I will raise it up." John then adds this commentary: "He was speaking of the temple of his body." In other words, Herod's temple is to be replaced by the body of Christ. A temple of lifeless stone will be replaced by a temple of living stone. This new temple of the body of Christ will not be fixed to a single geographical location, but will be a global temple located wherever two or three are gathered in the name of Jesus. In the New Covenant the chosen people are the human race and the holy land is the whole earth. In the Olivet Discourse Jesus gives the signs that will indicate that the temple age of ritual sacrifice and ethnic particularity is coming to an end.

In this talk, Jesus describes the tumultuous events of the AD 60s and 70s—famines, plagues, earthquakes, the persecution of Christians found in the book of Acts, the rise of false Messiahs, the Jewish war that began in the year 66, and finally the Roman siege of Jerusalem that began in February of 70 and ended with the destruction of the temple on August 10. The destruction of the temple officially marked the end of the temple age and confirmed that the rule of the Son of Man as envisioned by the prophet Daniel had indeed begun with Jesus' resurrection and ascension. The most important sentence in the Olivet Discourse is when Jesus says, "Truly I tell you, this generation will not pass away until all these things have happened." In other words, people who were alive when Jesus was teaching in Jerusalem would live to see all of these predictions about the end of the temple age come to pass. And that's exactly what happened.

Now is not the time to sift through the Olivet Discourse looking for signs by which to alarm people about the end of the world. Instead, now is the time for us to be about the good work of being the new temple, the temple of living stones that is the global body of Christ. Now is not the time to focus on Jesus' prediction of the destruction of Jerusalem—a prediction that came to pass almost two thousand years ago. Now is the time to work with Jesus in the construction of the New Jerusalem.

Lord Jesus, as you foretold, the old age of temple sacrifice has passed away with the end of the old temple. Help us now to participate in the new age you have inaugurated and to be living stones in your new temple. Amen.

Day 43

Holy Wednesday

Mark 14:1–9

Jesus Is Anointed in Bethany

On Wednesday evening of Holy Week Jesus is again in Bethany at the home of Lazarus, Martha, and Mary, where a dinner is given in his honor. During this dinner, Mary brings an alabaster jar filled with rare ointment of pure spikenard worth a year's wages and anoints Jesus' head with the entire contents. This is Mary's extravagant way of acknowledging that Jesus is the Messiah—the anointed King of Israel. Mary seems to be saying it's time for Jesus to be publicly acknowledged as Messiah—an event that will launch the revolution of God's kingdom.

But some of the disciples angrily scold Mary for her extravagance, saying, "Why was the ointment wasted in this way? It could have been sold for three hundred denarii, and the money given to the poor." And let's be honest, if we weren't already familiar with this story, we would expect Jesus to agree with the disciples in their rebuke of Mary. We would expect Jesus to say that perfume worth tens of thousands of dollars would be better spent on feeding and clothing the poor than by wasting it on a single moment of outrageous worship. We would be inclined to agree that this kind of worship is a misspent endeavor. But we would be wrong. Jesus defends Mary by calling what she did a beautiful thing. This leaves us with much to ponder.

Is it not true that there is no higher priority than doing good works of justice? Be careful, a devil lies down that road of reasoning. Jesus indeed teaches us to provide for the poor—this is part of the second commandment to love your neighbor as yourself. But the first command is to love God with all of your heart. And I am deeply skeptical that we can in the long-term fulfill the second commandment to love your neighbor as yourself if we are not formed by the first commandment to love God with all of your heart. Justice that is not rooted in the worship of God has no coherent foundation. As Fyodor Dostoevsky warned through his character Ivan Karamazov, "Without God all things are permitted."

So Jesus endorsed the extravagant anointing that Mary bestowed upon him. He even said that "wherever the gospel is preached in the whole world, what she has done will be told in memory of her." This emphasizes the truth that the gospel is not a salvation formula but the entire story of Jesus. Jesus also mysteriously says that Mary has anointed him for burial, which is certainly not what Mary was intending. Mary thought she was anointing Jesus for coronation, but Jesus says she anointed him for burial. Both are true. Jesus is the anointed King, and his coronation did launch the revolution of God's kingdom, but it also involved the burial of Jesus, because his coronation came by crucifixion and the revolution came by the cross. This is the gospel that is to be proclaimed in all the world.

Lord Jesus, may we follow the example of Mary of Bethany by wasting our lives on you. And when we are misunderstood and criticized for our extravagant worship, may we remember that you call it a beautiful thing. Amen.

DAY 44

MAUNDY THURSDAY

Luke 22:7–30

Jesus and the Last Supper

Today is Maundy (or mandate) Thursday, the day when Jesus at the Last Supper gave his disciples a new and supreme mandate to love one another. At the Last Supper Jesus re-appropriated the ancient Passover meal commemorating Israel's liberation from bondage in Egypt, giving us the sacramental meal of Communion by which we commemorate the Lord's death and partake of his body and blood. Of course the disciples didn't know this was the last supper before Jesus' suffering and death—they were still anticipating the arrival of the kingdom of God in the way of conventional conquest. Yet Jesus was explicit about this being the last meal of an old age, telling his disciples that he would not eat or drink again until the kingdom of God had come. And thus we see the significance of Jesus eating and drinking with his disciples following his resurrection!

Sadly, the poignancy of this final meal was marred by a dispute among the disciples over who would be regarded as the greatest in the coming kingdom. Once again, for the last time before his death, Jesus stresses to his obtuse disciples that what is counted as greatness in the empires of the world is not what is counted as greatness in the kingdom of God. Caesar and all his successors measure greatness by power—power to kill, power to obtain, power to control. But in the kingdom of Christ, greatness is measured by love, humility, and service. Jesus modeled this kingdom version of greatness when he washed his disciples' feet during the Last Supper.

Despite the disciples' inability to fully grasp what he was saying and doing, Jesus spoke warmly about how they had stayed with him through his trials. As a result they are to eat and drink at his table in his kingdom. (Notice that in Jesus' kingdom the central place of sacrament has shifted from temple to table.)

Finally Jesus says they will sit on twelve thrones and judge the reconfigured Israel that is the church. I often think of this passage of Scripture when I'm in a church that has statues or icons of the twelve Apostles ringing the interior dome, looking down upon the congregation. In the primacy we give to apostolic writings and practices, the Apostles do indeed judge the church.

On this Maundy Thursday, I hope you will be able to receive the sacrament of Communion—the means by which we participate in the body and blood of Jesus. To understand the full implications of the sacrament of Communion we need to remember that the body of Christ is three things: the corporal body of Jesus that was crucified and raised, the ecclesial body of Christ that is the church, and the Eucharistic body of Christ that is Communion. Through the sacrament of Communion all three aspects of the body of Christ are mysteriously connected. In the Eucharist we partake of the body and blood of Jesus that we, the church, might be the flesh and blood presence of Jesus Christ in the world.

Lord Jesus, as we partake of your body and blood on this holy day, may we be your flesh and blood presence in the world, and may our presence be characterized by love, humility, and service. Amen.

Day 45
Good Friday

Luke 23:1–56
The Crucifixion of Jesus

On Good Friday we think about one thing: the crucifixion of Jesus Christ. This is the epicenter of Christian faith. At the core of Christianity we don't find perennial religion, meditation techniques, or a course in ethics, but a crucifixion. This is the enduring scandal of the gospel. The gospel is not motivational talks about happy marriages, being debt free, and achieving your destiny. That all belongs to the broader world of proverbial wisdom, and it's fine as far as it goes, but it has little or nothing to do with the gospel. The gospel is about the cross and the cross is a scandal. When the Apostle Paul told the Corinthians that he had determined to know nothing among them except Jesus

Christ and him crucified, he admitted that the cross was often viewed as a scandal and folly. So be it. Any attempt to make Christianity less offensive and more palatable by de-emphasizing the cross is a betrayal of Jesus Christ himself. So today above all days we look unflinchingly at Christ crucified. To enter deep into the mystery of the cross is to encounter the greatest revelation of who God is. For being disguised under the disfigurement of an ugly crucifixion and death, Christ upon the cross is paradoxically the clearest revelation of who God is.

To interpret the meaning of the cross is more than a life's work—in fact, it has and will remain the work of the church for millennia. The cross is the ever-unfolding revelation of who God is, and it cannot be summed up in a simple formula. This is the bane of tidy atonement theories that seek to reduce the cross to a single meaning. The cross is many things:

It's the pinnacle of God's self-disclosure.

It's divine solidarity with all human suffering.

It's the shaming of principalities and powers.

It's the point from which the satan is driven out of the world.

It's the death by which Christ conquers Death.

It's the abolition of war and violence.

It's the supreme demonstration of the love of God.

It's the re-founding of the world around an axis of love.

It's the enduring model of co-suffering love we are to follow.

It's the eternal moment in which the sin of the world is forgiven.

The cross is not the appeasement of an angry and retributive god. The cross is not where Jesus saves us from God, but where Jesus reveals God as savior. The cross is not what God inflicts upon Jesus in order to forgive, but what God in Christ endures as he forgives. The cross is where the sin of the world coalesced into a hideous singularity so that it might be forgiven en masse. The cross is where the world violently sinned its sins in the body of the Son of God, and where he absorbed it all, praying, "Father, forgive them." The cross is both ugly and beautiful. It's as ugly as human sin and as beautiful as divine love—but in the end love and beauty win.

Lord Jesus, as we look at you on the cross, with your arms outstretched in proffered embrace, we pray, forgive us, Lord, for we know not what we do. Amen.

DAY 46
HOLY SATURDAY

John 19:31–42
Jesus in the Garden Tomb

And so on Holy Saturday, our forty-six day journey with Jesus through Lent comes to an end. Our long journey ends with Jesus laid to rest in a new tomb within the walled garden of Joseph of Arimathea near Golgotha. History and archeology suggest to us that in the time of Jesus, Golgotha was an abandoned quarry used as a garbage dump. So we could say it this way: Jesus, the stone rejected by the builders, was crucified in a quarry turned garbage dump, but he was buried as seed within a verdant garden. When Jesus is first seen alive in that garden on Easter morning, Mary Magdalene mistakes him for the gardener. But, in fact, it's no mistake at all. Jesus is the gardener who turns garbage dumps into gardens!

Jesus is not a **conductor** punching tickets for a train ride to heaven. Christian hope is not about getting from earth to heaven, it's about getting heaven to earth. Jesus is not a **lawyer** to get us out of a legal jam with an angry judge. God is not mad at sinners. Jesus told Mary to tell his disciples that his Father was their Father too! Jesus is not a **banker** making loans from his surplus righteousness. Modern people love economic metaphors, but these inevitably produce bad theology. Jesus is a **gardener!** A gardener cultivating resurrection life in all who will come to him. The conductor, lawyer, banker metaphors are mostly false, giving a distorted view of salvation. The gardener metaphor is beautiful as it faithfully depicts the process of salvation in our lives.

A gardener's work is earthy and intimate. Gardeners have their hands in the humus. (We are humans from the humus.) Conductors, lawyers and bankers are concerned with abstract and impersonal things like tickets, laws, and money. But gardeners handle living things with living hands. Jesus is not afraid to get his hands dirty in the humus of humanity. That Jesus is a gardener with a good heart and a green thumb should change your perspective. I promise you that your life is not so blighted that Jesus can't nurture you into something beautiful. The empty tomb is the open door that leads us away from the ugly world of Gehennas and garbage dumbs and back home to the God-intended garden.

No one has captured the idea of Easter as the inauguration of a new world with Christ as the gardener better than G.K. Chesterton. I always anticipate Easter by reading this passage from *The Everlasting Man*.

> On the third day the friends of Christ coming at daybreak to the place found the grave empty and the stone rolled away. In varying ways they realized the new wonder; the world had died in the night. What they were looking at was the first day of a new creation, with a new heaven and a new earth; and in a semblance of a gardener God walked again in the garden, in the cool not of the evening but the dawn.

Lord Jesus, on this holy day of quiet rest, we await your resurrection when we will encounter you walking in the garden in the divine guise of the gardener. Amen.

Manufactured by Amazon.ca
Bolton, ON

10997192R00116